SUNDAY IN CENTREVILLE

THE BATTLE OF BULL RUN, 1861

SUNDAY IN CENTREVILLE

THE BATTLE OF BULL RUN, 1861

by G. ALLEN FOSTER

illustrated by HAROLD BERSON

DAVID WHITE *NEW YORK*

BY THE SAME AUTHOR

COMMUNICATION: From Primitive Tom Toms to Telstar

THE EYES AND EARS OF THE CIVIL WAR

IMPEACHED: The President Who Almost Lost His Job

VOTES FOR WOMEN

Second Printing
Text copyright © 1971 David White, Inc.
Illustrations copyright © 1971 David White, Inc.

Library of Congress Catalog Card Number: 73—129214

SBN 87250—243—0 (Trade)
SBN 87250—441—7 (Library)

David White, Inc., publishers
60 East 55th Street New York, New York 10022

Printed in the United States of America

CONTENTS

v

FOREWORD

THE battle of Bull Run of July 21, 1861, the first important action in the Civil War, led to the North's sudden, sharp realization that the South was not the weak antagonist that had been anticipated.

What many expected to be only a short, diverting camping trip turned into a gray nightmare of death and mutilation. The eager Union volunteers from mills, farms, stores, and government offices, who had looked forward to a few exciting months away from tedious jobs, quickly became weary, dirty, despairing men.

In this first major confrontation between the armies of the Union and the Confederacy, the fighting men on both sides were amateurs, with little or no training. There were some able military leaders, but there were also a number of inexperienced, inept fumblers. Many mistakes were made, and instead of the expected short war, there followed an agonizing four years of bloodletting. When it was over, 800,000 had died.

SUNDAY IN CENTREVILLE

THE BATTLE OF BULL RUN, 1861

INTRODUCTION

WHY DID IT HAPPEN?

ALTHOUGH history books before the 1920's give slavery and secession as the issues of the American Civil War, later historians considered this too simple an explanation. Certainly secession led to violence, and the slaves were "freed" as a result of the war, but the bitter confrontation between the states was also due to the deep differences in the cultural and economic backgrounds of the industrial North and agricultural South.

Even though President Lincoln was concerned about slavery and wanted to see it abolished, he felt that the paramount issue was to keep the Union together. When he issued his appeal for 75,000 volunteers on April 15, 1861, nine Southern states had already seceded. But he had waited before calling the troops until the South had become the aggressor by firing on Fort Sumter. It is significant to note, too, that until the bombardment of Fort Sumter, President Lincoln had made no effort to take over federal forts and military installations along the Gulf Coast and in Texas, some of which were in the hands of the seceded states.

There was, of course, another side to secession. Technically, the Southern states, which had been among the original thirteen colonies, did not secede at all. They called conventions which rescinded the ordinances by which they had ratified the Constitution. The greatest legal minds in the South believed that these states had a right to withdraw their ratification of the Constitution, and that the Founding Fathers had held that view when the document was ratified. President Buchanan considered that he had no right to prevent secession.

As for slavery, Abraham Lincoln, in a letter to Horace Greeley, said that he would forget about it if this would save the Union. Until the Emancipation Proclamation of 1863, slaves were still owned in Maryland, Kentucky and Missouri, states which did not secede. In the early years of the war, slave owners were permitted to come through the lines and into federal army encampments under flags of truce, to identify and retrieve escaped slaves. The Emancipation Proclamation was, at the time, a military and political instrument as much as it was a humane document. With the 1864 presidential election coming up, emancipation would draw the Abolitionist vote to Lincoln, who believed that he could not win without it. Militarily, the Proclamation discouraged slaves from working on Confederate fortifications or railroads and at arsenals.

By 1861, in state after state, slavery was becoming unprofitable. Even more hated in the South than Harriet Beecher Stowe's *Uncle Tom's Cabin* was a book by a North Carolinian, Hinton Rowan Helper's *The Impending Crisis* (1857), in which he proved by cold statistics that slavery was economically strangling the South.

Helper said that slavery had bound the South to an agrarian economy. This, he said, had given the North a chance to expand industrially until it had economic superiority over the South. The North, he pointed out, imported skilled labor from Europe or trained native labor to operate machines, while the South had not trained its slaves in mechanical skills and therefore had no industry.

Helper drove his point home by saying that a Southern baby at birth was put in swaddling clothes made in a Massachusetts textile mill; his hobby horse was made in Maine; as a young man, he "sowed his wild oats" in New York City; his bride's wedding ring came from Rhode Island; his Colt revolver was made in Hartford, Connecticut; his burial shroud was woven in New Jersey, and his tombstone was quarried in Vermont.

As damnable as the institution was, slavery of necessity included the most

2

expensive social security system ever devised. A healthy young black couple cost between $2,400 and $3,000. They had to be fed reasonably well to protect the owner's investment. When the couple had children, the youngsters had to be cared for until they grew old enough to work or be sold. If one or both of the couple became ill, they had to have medical attention. When they were too old to work, the slave owner had to care for them until they died.

The division which led to the Civil War was basic. The Southerner had brought from England, or, if he lived in Louisiana, from France, a tradition of gracious living, a degree of independence from government and a consciousness of social position. To be called a gentleman, one must be a clergyman, a lawyer, a soldier or a planter. A doctor possibly might qualify, but seldom a banker, and never a manufacturer.

While the South brought its traditions from across the Atlantic, the North brought customs but not traditions. The definition of a gentleman was broader. No one was interested in what his family had been in England. But it meant a good deal if an ancestor had fought in the Revolution. And if you lived in Massachusetts, it was important to have had a relative aboard the *Mayflower*. The Congregational minister was automatically a gentleman, as was the schoolmaster, and generally the same man had both roles in the Northern colonies. Continuing from there, social position was assessed by education, money, achievement and political power. If the owner of a textile mill was a church deacon, a member of the school board, a college graduate, a director of the bank, and maybe even a member of the state legislature, he was a gentleman.

It is very possible that if slave labor had been profitable in early New England, there might have been few Abolitionists. The federal census of 1790 for New Hampshire counted sixteen slaves, all in Portsmouth, then the capital of the state, and obviously house servants. On the rocky farms of New England, with a short growing season, a farmer with 300 acres of land could not afford to feed and clothe a slave. Besides, a recently imported African could hardly

3

work efficiently in three feet of snow with the temperature at 35 degrees below zero. No wonder this farmer envied the Louisiana sugar planter who owned 5,000 acres and 1,500 slaves to work them, while he served as colonel of the Louisiana Tigers (a militia regiment), read the classics in his generously stocked library, served as vestryman in the Episcopal Church and president of the Plaquemines Parish Agricultural Society.

Northerners and Southerners saw government, at all levels, through different glasses. Northerners considered the states subordinate to the federal government. Southerners regarded themselves as citizens of their sovereign states first and held the view that the states permitted the federal government to exist.

Within the Southern states, the county was the most powerful political unit below the state. Because of the size of the plantations, settlements were often far apart. If there was crime, the plantation owner looked to the county sheriff, rather than to the village constable, even if there was such an officer. In the North, particularly in New England, the town was the strongest unit of government within the state. Annually, on the second Tuesday of March, every registered voter was summoned to attend the Town Meeting. There, every item of the town's budget was argued and voted on by the entire citizenry. Any voter could demand recognition and speak as long as he chose on any pertinent subject. Because Southerners did not run their local affairs the same way, New Englanders believed them to be undemocratic.

Since their sovereign states held their first loyalty, Southerners were more inclined than Northerners to elect able representatives to the state legislatures. Washington, Lee, Patrick Henry, Jefferson, Madison and Monroe started their public careers in the Virginia legislature. The plantation owner who could debate constitutional law and quote Plato, and who could turn over the supervision of his fields to an overseer while the legislature was in session, made an attractive candidate.

This is not to say that political giants did not begin their careers in the

Northern legislatures, but the men of outstanding ability were more likely to be busy making money and to feel that they could not take time away from their businesses to sit through a long legislative session. Here again there was friction between two sets of values.

But the greatest force driving the South to secession, and then to war, was discouragement. The South, until perhaps 1856, had held the reins in the federal government. In 1800, Virginia was the most populous state in the Union. By 1849 she had provided six presidents. From 1790 to 1860, no presidential nominee could be elected without the general approval of the South. Franklin Pierce and James Buchanan were the last examples of this dominance.

But, beginning in the 1840's, the population trend in the North, and especially in the West (now the Middle West), began to challenge the governmental influence of the South. Immigrants began pouring into northeastern cities, generally strengthening the urban Democratic machines. New York City had passed Boston in population, but Boston was bursting with new Irish citizens. At the same time, cheap, fertile land in Iowa, Illinois, Indiana, Michigan and Wisconsin was drawing farmers from the rocky hills of Maine, New Hampshire, Vermont and up-state New York. Then the California gold rush of 1849 drew enough easterners to bring that formerly Mexican territory in as a state. The result was that every decennial census increased the North's representation in Congress. By 1860, the only branch of the government in which the South had the decisive voice was the Supreme Court.

Because of a lack of communication between the North and South the two regions had developed stereotypes, each equally repugnant to the people of the other region. To the Northerner, the typical Southerner was a planter who whipped his slaves, sold off their children and watched his cotton grow, while he lounged on the front porch of his mansion with a mint julep in his hand. He was against progress because that would entail federal funds. Like John C. Calhoun, and later Jefferson Davis, when he was Senator from Mississippi, he opposed the government's putting navigation buoys on the Mississippi, because this was an invasion of "states' rights." Buoys were the responsibility of the states along the river. If one state did not buoy its section of the river and boats were sunk by hidden snags that was just "tough luck."

Furthermore, the average planter was a poor businessman. He spent too much time in his private library reading the *Federalist Papers,* while defaulting on loans to New York banks. Southern young men occupied themselves with barbecues, fox hunts, drinking, gambling and courting Southern belles in the midst of magnolia and honeysuckle instead of learning to manage a factory, a bank or a department store. Southerners were hot-heads and emotionally unstable. "Look, they're still fighting duels over some fool thing called 'honor.' "

To the equally myopic Southerner, the Northerner was a busybody and a meddler who wanted everyone in the United States to act and govern himself as he did. He looked down on the South because it had plantations instead of factories. Had the Northerner ever stopped to think how a magnolia tree would look in a mill yard? The North was governed by white trash not fit to vote, the Southerners declared with scorn. New Englanders cried out against slavery, but the textile fortunes of New Hampshire, Massachusetts and Rhode Island had been made possible by Southern cotton, produced by slave labor.

The South overestimated the abolition sentiment in the North. It overlooked the anti-abolition riots in many Northern communities. It regarded Lincoln's election as a vindication of the Abolitionists and believed that, with the Republican Party in control, slavery would be abolished upon his inauguration.

What irked the Southerners most was the Abolitionists' "higher law"—an ethic above the Constitution. The Constitution recognized slavery. The Supreme Court had ruled in the Dred Scott decision that runaway slaves, if apprehended, must be returned to their owners. Yet the Underground Railroad flourished, ignored by Northern law-enforcement officers, in defiance of federal law. If the North could flout the Constitution on slavery, why not in other areas, the South asked.

Then there was the matter of John Brown. In some parts of the North, especially among the Abolitionists, he was a saint. To the South he was a dangerous revolutionary. Brown, a ne'er-do-well who had failed at both business and farming, decided to try his luck once more by moving to Kansas. It was just at the time that the Missouri Compromise, passed by Congress on May 30, 1854, was to take effect. Under its provisions, the territories of Missouri and Kansas were to decide by popular vote whether they would enter the Union as slave or free states.

By the time John Brown left for Kansas, he had become a radical Abolitionist. He subscribed to William Lloyd Garrison's *Liberator* and read every piece of Abolitionist propaganda he could lay his hands on. On arriving in Kansas, Brown learned that, in a referendum, Missouri would vote heavily for slavery. There were 50,000 slaves in the territory at the time. He also found that the slave owners in Missouri were determined that Kansas should not be taken over by the Abolitionists who were arriving in droves. Kansas, as a free state, would provide a perfect escape route for runaway slaves.

When Southerners began pouring into Kansas, armed conflict was inevitable. Soon the shooting began, and Brown, a violent man, appealed to his Northern friends for help. It came in the form of boxes labeled "Bibles." The Southerners were soon calling the Sharps carbines which the boxes contained "Beecher's Bibles," since most of the money for buying them was raised by the famous preacher Henry Ward Beecher. This was regarded as another example of Northern interference in Southern affairs.

It took several years for John Brown to finance and organize his raid on Harper's Ferry, Virginia. On Sunday, October 15, 1859, Brown led his attack on the United States Arsenal. He was met by a mob of private citizens, many of them arsenal employees who came out with rifles they had just made. Several men were killed on both sides. When Colonel Robert E. Lee arrived from Washington with a detachment of marines, most of those who were barricaded with Brown in the Arsenal engine house were killed, including Brown's son, Watson. John Brown was hanged by the state of Virginia.

The South was outraged by the whole situation, insisting that a wild-eyed fanatic had been financed by Northern Abolitionists. But worse than that, these same Abolitionists and other Northerners were now singing: "John Brown's body lies a-moldering in the grave, but his soul goes marching on."

Hot-headed Southern orators and editors had been urging secession for years. John Brown was meat for their stew. In 1850, soon after the Mexican War, a convention of secessionists was held in Nashville, Tennessee. It proposed the secession of the Southern states and the annexation of Texas to the new confederation, splitting it into several states. Most vocal at this convention were Jefferson Davis and Albert Gallatin Brown, both of Mississippi, as well as William Lowndes Yancy of Alabama and Robert Rhett of South Carolina. Also present were Roger Pryor and Edward A. Pollard of the Richmond *Examiner,* as well as other editors, and the South was bombarded daily with reports of real or suspected crimes of the North against the South. The predicted economic submersion of the South, and a genuine belief that the South could subsist as an agrarian economy, encouraged a conviction that the South could withdraw from the Union peaceably and form an independent nation. When Governor Francis Wilkinson Pickens of South Carolina, after secession of the state, wanted to take over all United States property in his state, including the forts in Charleston harbor, Fort Sumter was occupied by U.S. troops under Robert Anderson. This action threw a new light on the situation and was all that was needed to ignite the fuse.

CHAPTER ONE

"I DO SOLEMNLY SWEAR..."

IT was a beautiful, cool, sunny day that eighteenth of February, 1861. There was just enough breeze to rustle the hoop skirts of the Southern belles lining the sidewalk of Dexter Avenue in Montgomery, Alabama. The parade swung up the hill to the state capitol. There was a brass band in red uniforms, the gleaming horns with their bells uniformly pointed over the left shoulders of the players. The band was playing "The Bonnie Blue Flag," a song which had first been sung to a Jackson, Mississippi, theater audience a few weeks before by an entertainer named Harry McArthy. Then came a regiment of Alabama militia, a hand-pumped fire engine and hose reel, the members of the Provisional Congress, and finally a highly polished carriage carrying Jefferson Davis and Alexander H. Stephens, President-elect and Vice-President-elect of the Confederate States of America.

Arriving at the Capitol, the Provisional Congress went inside where the oath of office was administered to Davis and Stephens by the Chief Justice of the

Alabama Supreme Court. Then the assemblage repaired to the steps of the Capitol for the inaugural address.

Considering the emotional tension of the moment, the first and only President of the Confederacy delivered a surprisingly moderate address, in no way inflammatory. At the outset Davis said:

"Our present political position has been achieved in a manner unprecedented in the history of nations. It illustrates the American idea that governments rest on the consent of the governed, and that it is the right of the people to alter or abolish them at will whenever they become destructive of the ends for which they are established. . . .

"Sustained by the consciousness that the transition from the former Union to the Confederacy has not proceeded from a disregard on our part of just obligations, or any failure to perform every constitutional duty, moved by no interest or passion to invade the rights of others, anxious to cultivate peace and commerce with all nations, if we may not hope to avoid war, we may at least expect that posterity will acquit us of having needlessly engaged in it. Doubly justified by the absence of any wrong on our part, and by wanton aggression on the part of others, there can be no doubt that the courage and patriotism of the Confederate States will be found equal to any measure of defense which their honor and security may require."

Jefferson Davis had become President of the Confederacy by accident. He had not wanted the office, and his home state of Mississippi had not wanted him to have it. In Mississippi, Davis was idolized for his expert command of the first Mississippi Infantry in the Mexican War of 1846–47. With this experience and a West Point diploma, Mississippi wanted Davis to be general-in-chief of the new Confederate Army. The provisional president would serve only one year, or until a permanent constitution could be drafted. No one believed a war with the North could last that long. When the war was over, Davis would

Jefferson Davis

emulate George Washington and exchange his epaulets for the broadcloth of the presidency.

The Provisional Congress, which was to draft a provisional constitution and elect a provisional president, was dominated by the Georgia delegation. (Virginia and North Carolina had not then seceded.) In that delegation were the three strongest candidates for the presidency: Alexander Stephens, Howell Cobb and Robert Toombs. Stephens, in his forties, weighed ninety pounds, was five feet tall and had never shaved. Even on the hottest days, he always wore a long woolen overcoat. But "Little Alec" Stephens had been considered one of the most learned constitutional authorities in the former United States.

Both Stephens and Cobb had opposed the secession of Georgia. The wealthy Cobb had been a Whig congressman and had never joined the Democratic Party after the Whig demise. He had been elected Speaker of the U.S. House of Representatives in 1849. In the election of 1860, Cobb and Stephens had formed the Constitutional Union Party in Georgia in an effort to block secession. Cobb was the least popular of the so-called Georgia Triumvirate.

Robert Toombs was the favorite of the Georgia delegation. He was a mountain of a man with thick sensuous lips and hair that fell nearly to his shoulders. In the U.S. Senate he had been classed with Daniel Webster both as an orator and as a consumer of hard liquor.

The night before the Provisional Congress, meeting in Montgomery, was to elect a president, word was passed from delegation to delegation that Georgia would vote solidly for Howell Cobb. If this were true, the choice would not be popular with the other states. Then one delegate reported that he had just seen Robert Toombs coming out of a hotel bar, walking somewhat unsteadily. He could hardly be a candidate for president. The name of Jefferson Davis came up, and it was decided that Davis should be nominated to head off Cobb. If Cobb's nomination was not unanimous, he would certainly withdraw. It was agreed that Davis was the best available candidate. He was wealthy, with a brilliant record in the U.S. Senate; he had been a hero of the Mexican War and had served as Secretary of War under Franklin Pierce. Mississippi still wanted its favorite son to be general-in-chief, but it could not deny him the presidency if the other states wanted him.

The next morning, state after state voted for Jefferson Davis. Then the clerk called "Georgia," and the delegation chairman, obviously embarrassed, moved to make Davis's election unanimous. The truth became known when the Congress recessed. Georgia had intended to nominate Robert Toombs!

The sun shone on Washington on March 4, 1861, as it had shone on Montgomery in February, but there was a raw, biting wind that chilled the bones and whipped up great clouds of dust on still-unpaved Pennsylvania Avenue. It was noon, a bit behind schedule, when three companies of regular infantry drew up in front of Willard's Hotel. There was the usual bustle of officialdom familiar to today's television viewers on Inauguration Day. Word was passed down the Avenue and the cavalry drew its sabers and snapped to "present ARMS." The marine band played four ruffles and flourishes and "Hail to the Chief." Mr. Lincoln and President Buchanan emerged from the hotel, arm in arm. "Old Buck" wore an air of obvious relief that his sorely troubled administration would be over in an hour.

The cavalcade proceeded toward the Capitol. Cavalry, riding on each side of the carriage, screened the President and the President-elect from any potential assassin on the sidewalks. Never had Washington seen such security precautions; they were provided because there had been rumors that Abraham Lincoln would be shot before he could take the oath of office.

Instead of being handled by the usual political chairman of the Inaugural Committee, all arrangements were in the hands of General of the Army Winfield Scott. There were cannon in all of Washington's famous circles, placed where they could sweep the avenues with cannister shot if necessary. There were sharpshooters on the roofs of all Pennsylvania Avenue buildings and in many windows. Down on the street, the crowds were infiltrated by Pinkerton detectives. (During Lincoln's administration Allan Pinkerton was to organize the first U.S. Secret Service.)

The cavalcade to the Capitol was the nineteenth-century's usual display of panoply. The ride to the oath-taking was more colorful and impressive than in the Kennedy-Johnson-Nixon era. The President-elect has gone to his inauguration with only a police escort in this later period, leaving the grand pageant for the afternoon.

Lincoln and Buchanan were escorted by the District of Columbia militia, battalions of regular infantry, cavalry, marines, a few floats and of course the marine band. At the Capitol, the party entered the Senate Chamber where Hannibal Hamlin of Maine, a former Democrat, was sworn in as Vice-President. Then the Senate, the House, the Supreme Court and Buchanan's Cabinet moved to the platform erected over the east steps of the Capitol. President Buchanan and Lincoln were escorted by Senator Edward D. Baker of Oregon, who, as a volunteer officer, would soon be killed in the abortive battle of Ball's Bluff. As the crowd watched Lincoln and his party descend the steps, it could also see the muzzle of a sharpshooter's rifle protruding from every window above.

Then came an embarrassing moment. Dictated by custom rather than infirmity, Lincoln was carrying a gold-headed cane in addition to his elegant stovepipe hat. When he approached the speaker's table, he faced the problem of where to place these items. The cane went under the table, but what could he do with the hat? The platform of rough, unplaned pine boards was not meant for a silk hat. Also there was that stiff March wind which might deposit the hat amid the crowd where it would be a prized souvenir. Lincoln was obviously upset and perplexed. His aplomb was saved by his arch rival and long-time

Abraham Lincoln

political enemy. Senator Stephen A. Douglas of Illinois came forward, took Lincoln's stovepipe hat and held it in his lap during the inaugural rites.

Lincoln's inaugural address, like that of Jefferson Davis, was moderate in tone. "We are not enemies, but friends. We must not be enemies. Though passion may be strained, it must not break our bonds of affection. The mystic chords of memory which stretch from every battlefield and patriot grave to every loved hearthstone, all over our broad land, will swell to the chorus of the Union when again touched, as surely they will be, by the better angels of our nature. . . ."

For the second time that March 4, ruffles and flourishes and "Hail to the Chief." The artillery on the Capitol Plaza and at the Navy Yard crashed out the traditional twenty-one-gun salute. Cavalry escorted the new President to the White House where there was an hour-long reception. Then without further fanfare, Lincoln and his Cabinet got down to business behind locked doors. There was a cursory assessment of the nation's military capabilities (Secretaries Simon Cameron and Gideon Welles), the condition of the Treasury (Secretary Salmon P. Chase), transportation, the Navy Yard (Secretary Welles) and the current disposition of naval vessels and army units.

That night President Abraham Lincoln climbed the steep staircase to the family quarters on the second floor of the White House and went to bed, wrapped in a knee-length nightshirt and deep gloom.

CHAPTER TWO

IT CAN'T HAPPEN HERE

WITH the inauguration of Jefferson Davis as President of the Confederate States of America, the Confederate Congress settled down to draft a permanent constitution. By March 11, this had been completed and ratified. The document was almost a verbatim copy of the United States Constitution with one notable exception. Many a President of the United States has since wished that he could use that exception. The Confederate Constitution provided that the President could veto one item in an appropriation bill without vetoing the whole bill. No United States President has ever been able to do that.

The Constitution ratified, President Davis turned his attention to the military condition of the Confederacy. Up to this point no military action had been taken by the seceded states or by the Confederacy, which had no army or navy. Davis had sent commissioners to Washington to discuss with President Lincoln a Confederate take-over of all U.S. military installations in the South. At the same time, he asked his Congress for legislation to provide that, in case the Washington negotiations failed (which they did), the installations should be seized by the militia of each state concerned, but that all equipment taken should be turned over to the central government for the beginnings of an army and navy. In no way did Davis hint at a threatening war. He was simply doing his duty, he said, in providing for a prudent defense.

A few days later, Davis asked Leroy Pope Walker, his Secretary of War, to submit a budget for the "Army of the Confederate States" which would include a modest amount for the purchase of weapons in Europe. Davis admitted in his message to Congress that he saw little hope of recruiting an army up to the strength projected in Walker's budget, and he recommended that the balance of the appropriation be held in reserve to compensate state militia troops if they were needed at any time.

After passing a few laws to implement the new Constitution, the Confederate Congress adjourned and went home, without a single Rebel yell.

In Washington, where the new Congress convened following Lincoln's inauguration, there was an air of quiet optimism. With most of the Southern Representatives absent, the House and Senate were safely Republican. Only in the Supreme Court did the Democrats have control. At a Washington dinner of the New England Society, Secretary of State William Henry Seward predicted that every difference with the South would be settled in sixty days.

Washington could not bring itself to realize that the nation had really become divided. It was hard to believe that the American flag no longer flew over Southern post offices or state capitols. The authority of the federal government had never been challenged except in small local skirmishes such as Shays' Rebellion in Massachusetts (September 26, 1786), the short-lived Whiskey Rebellion in Pennsylvania (August 7, 1794), John Brown's recent raid on Harper's Ferry (October 18, 1859). Even after Fort Sumter at Charleston, South Carolina, had been placed under the guns of the South Carolina Militia with demands that the United States hand over the installation, the Washington correspondents of the New York *Tribune* were telegraphing Horace Greeley that Lincoln seemed to favor a quiet evacuation of the fort on the recommendation of General-in-Chief Winfield Scott.

In Congress, the Democrats, although in a minority, were vocal in their demands that the President clearly state his position toward the new Confederacy. Virginia and North Carolina had not yet seceded and so had Congressional representation. The border states, Maryland, Delaware, Kentucky and Missouri, had strong Democratic delegations.

Senator Stephen A. Douglas of Illinois, although a Union man to the last, stated his attitude toward the status of the Confederacy: "We certainly cannot justify the holding of the forts here, much less the recapturing of those which have been taken, unless we intend to reduce those states themselves into subjugation. . . . We cannot deny that there is a Southern Confederacy, de facto, in existence, with its capital at Montgomery. We may regret it, I regret it most profoundly, but I cannot deny the truth of the fact, painful and mortifying as it is."

At this same time, Confederate Vice-President Alexander Stephens issued a statement congratulating the seceded states on their bloodless revolution, reminding his public that the population of the Confederacy was greater than that of the thirteen colonies at the time of the Revolution and that the territory of the Confederacy was greater than France, Spain, Portugal and the British Isles combined.

In the North, there was almost a complete lack of belligerence, as many Northern leaders accepted the presence of the Confederacy and began issuing suggestions for healing the breach and reuniting the nation. A National Society for Promoting Unity was formed, with Samuel F. B. Morse, the inventor of the telegraph, as its president. The society preached that the North should change its attitude and join with the South in the belief that slavery was ordained by God.

William Howard Russell, foreign correspondent of the London *Times,* ar-

Fort Sumter

rived in Washington in the middle of March. He had been sent to report the possibilities of war and to cover the conflict if it occurred. His coverage of the war was brief, since he found it wise to leave this country after his report of the battle of Bull Run. He had the audacity to tell the truth. As a world traveler and the representative of the most powerful newspaper in the world at the time, Russell soon had access to the White House, the State Department, the embassies and many members of Congress. Few of his acquaintances thought there would be a war, and there was strong sentiment for appeasing the South.

The chief controversy, and that was mild for the most part, was what action the President should take if the Confederacy seized Fort Pickens, Fort Sumter and other federal installations. One argument contended that the forts had been constructed with taxes provided partly by the South, and that three federal installations in the South should be turned over to the Confederate government as its rightful due. After all, an independent nation required coastal defenses, and turning over the forts would certainly avoid war.

The other argument was that the forts were federal property, that the President had taken an oath to protect federal property and that he must abide by his oath.

Neither side argued vehemently or volubly, because neither side knew President Lincoln's position at the time, if he knew it himself.

On April 4, Russell had a long press conference with Secretary of State Seward whom he found in a state of depression. Seward told Russell that the apparent indecision of the Lincoln administration was actually its inability to enforce a decision if it made one. Former Secretary of War John Buchanan Floyd, a secessionist, had not only transferred 135,000 rifles to Southern arsenals while he was in office but had sent most of the U.S. Army, consisting of only 12,000 men, to Texas where they were as far as possible from Washington and could be overwhelmed enroute by Southern militia. In addition, Secretary of the Navy Isaac Toucey, a Connecticut resident but a Southern sympathizer, had, under President Buchanan, scattered most of the U.S. Navy's little, wooden fleet around the world on "courtesy visits" so that it might be well out of the way in case of trouble. Seward was concerned too, about the defection of many of the army's best officers to the Confederacy.

But on one point Seward was evasive with Russell, as he had been with everyone else who brought up the subject of the Confederate Commissioners. A week after his inauguration at Montgomery, Jefferson Davis sent the following message to the Confederate Congress: "I hereby transmit for the advice of the Congress the following nominations of Commissioners to the United States in accordance with the resolution of Congress providing for such commissions and declaratory of the purposes thereof: A. B. Roman of Louisiana; M. J. Crawford of Georgia; John Forsyth of Alabama."

The purposes of the commission referred to in the resolution were ". . . negotiating friendly relations with that government [the United States] and the Confederate States of America, and for the settlement of all questions of disagreement between the two governments upon principles of right, justice, equity and good faith."

On February 27, 1861, President Davis had addressed a letter to President Lincoln transmitting the credentials of the Confederate Commissioners. Davis, whether naively or not, believed in all sincerity that he was sending accredited representatives of a de facto nation to another nation to settle international problems, not simply trying to patch up differences between the seceding states and the North. As might be expected, Lincoln did not reply to the Davis letter, because to do so would have violated a principle to which Lincoln adhered throughout the war and pledged his successor, Vice-President Andrew Johnson, to continue.

This principle was the refusal to admit the existence of the Confederate States of America. He stoutly maintained that, at that time, nine Southern states were in rebellion against their country; that they had illegally seized federal property and interfered with shipping. He was perfectly willing to negotiate with states individually, adjust differences and admit them back into the Union. To be consistent in this attitude, he could not deal with the Confederacy.

When the Confederate Commissioners arrived in Washington, they immediately applied for an appointment with Secretary of State Seward through whom they would request an audience with Lincoln. Seward took his time in replying to the Commissioners while he held several conferences with his chief. Then Seward's reply came: Neither he nor the President would receive the Commissioners. But in the area now known as "Foggy Bottom," there are several mysteries which have never been clarified. The Confederate Commissioners saw somebody; otherwise they would have gone home. Somebody gave them the impression that if they stayed around awhile, everything would work out to their satisfaction. And so they stayed on and on with not even a hint from the White House or the Secretary of State.

The mystery is further deepened by the disclosures of New York *Tribune* editor, Horace Greeley, in his *American Conflict*: ". . . Col. G. W. Lay, an aide of General Scott, had visited Charleston on March 20, and had had a long interview with Governor Pickens and General Beauregard, with reference, it was said, to the terms on which Fort Sumter should be evacuated, if at all. The 25th brought to Charleston Col. Ward H. Lamon, a confidential agent of the President, who, after an interview with the Confederate authorities, was permitted to visit the fort [Sumter], and hold unrestricted intercourse with Major Anderson [commandant of the fort], who apprised the Government through him [Lamon] that their scanty stock of provisions would suffice his little garrison only till the middle of April. Col. Lamon returned immediately to Washington, and was said to have reported there that, in Major Anderson's opinion, as well as his own, the relief of the fortress was impracticable."

Here we appear to have a very confusing and conflicting situation. Lincoln and Seward had refused to receive the Confederate Commissioners, because to

do so would be tantamount to recognizing the Confederacy. But Colonel Lay, representing the United States, had negotiated with Pierre Gustave Toufant Beauregard, general of the Confederate Army, and Ward Lamon, representing the President of the United States, had conferred with the Confederate authorities at Charleston.

The rest is textbook history. The Commissioners had cooled their heels long enough and went home. To the surprise of those who had been "in the know," Lincoln ordered Fort Sumter supplied with food and ammunition. The supply ship was repulsed by the Charleston shore batteries. Then Lieutenant Talbot, an officer under Major Anderson, was permitted by the Confederates to go to Washington to report that the fort's food supply would not hold out three days. Talbot returned to Charleston with a letter from the State Department informing Governor Pickens that Sumter would be relieved at all costs. Pickens and Beauregard telegraphed this information to the Confederate Secretary of War, Leroy Walker. The reply was "Demand the prompt surrender of the fort or reduce it." This was on April 10. On April 12, Edmund Ruffin, a trembling old veteran of the War of 1812, pulled the lanyard of a large Whitworth naval cannon and fired the second "shot heard 'round the world." That night, President Jefferson Davis sent out a call for an emergency session of the Confederate Congress. On April 15 President Abraham Lincoln issued his proclamation calling up 75,000 troops for three months. It could happen here.

CHAPTER THREE

FATHER 'N' I WENT DOWN TO CAMP

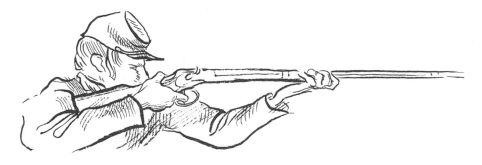

Father 'n' I went down to camp,
Along with Cap'n Goodwin,
And there we saw the men and boys,
As thick as hasty puddin'.
"Yankee Doodle"

CAPTAIN Goodwin was presumably on his way to the annual muster of his state militia company which took all of one day and completed the company's military training for a year. It was with this training and tradition that the two opposing armies faced each other at Bull Run on July 21, 1861.

On January 18, 1790, Henry Knox, a leading general in the Revolution, then Secretary of War under George Washington, sent the President his plan for a national militia organized by states. He said that a well-trained militia would avoid "the vices of a standing army."

Secretary Knox wrote:

"The following plan is formed on these general principles:

"*First,* that it is the indispensable duty of every nation to establish all necessary institutions for its own protection and defense. *Secondly,* that it is a capital security to a free state for the great body of people to possess a competent knowledge of the military art. *Thirdly,* that this knowledge cannot be attained in the present state of society, but by establishing adequate institutions for the military education of youth, and that the knowledge acquired herein should be diffused throughout the community by the principles of rotation. *Fourthly,* that every man of the proper age and ability of body is firmly bound by the social compact to perform personally his proportion of military duty for the defense of the estate. *Fifthly,* that all men of military age should be armed, enrolled, and held responsible for different degrees of military service. *And sixthly,* that, agreeable to the Constitution, the United States are to provide for organizing, arming and disciplining the militia, and for governing such part of them as may be employed in the services of the United States; reserving to the states, respectively, the appointment of officers and the authority of training the militia according to the discipline prescribed by Congress."

In his third provision regarding the training of youth in military science, Secretary Knox was apparently thinking of a future U.S. Military Academy which would train young officers who would then return to their states and train the militia. This, of course, never happened. By 1861, the only trained officers in the militia were West Point graduates who had resigned their commissions after a few years in the Regular Army, had gone into business and become militia officers. And these were few, although they included future generals Ulysses S. Grant, George Brinton McClellan and Ambrose Everett Burnside.

Knox's plan, which was accepted, also was vague on the authority of the United States over the state militia regiments in time of war. In the War of 1812, the War Department *requested* the governor of Vermont to send a regiment of Vermont militia to Niagara Falls where the American forces were outnumbered. The governor sent the regiment, but before it reached its destination, he had changed his mind and recalled it.

In the Mexican War of 1846–47, the Southern states provided their quotas of men, but in New England, where the war was unpopular, the governors sent no troops, and Secretary of War William Marcy had learned to plead with New Hampshire's Franklin Pierce, the future President, to recruit personally a New England Brigade which would be sworn into the Regular Army. Pierce was never able to bring the brigade up to full strength, but he commanded it with distinction. And it must be remembered that after the bombardment of Fort Sumter, President Lincoln sent out a *call* for 75,000 volunteer troops. He did not, as Commander-in-Chief, order any governor to send him the needed regiments.

Secretary Knox had also prescribed that the militia officers be appointed by the states. It worked that way in theory but not in practice. Here is how militia companies and regiments were formed, armed and officered. The names and places are fictitious but the circumstances are factual.

Jonathan Walcott lived in Litchfield, Connecticut, and came from Revolutionary War stock. He was a lawyer, a member of the state legislature, master of the Omega Lodge of Free and Accepted Masons, deacon of the Congregational Church, had served three terms as selectman and was captain of the Eagle Hose Company. He was a powerful man, both bodily and politically. He was tall, broad-shouldered, and stood out in a crowd. He still had his father's Revolutionary War sword.

One Sunday after church, some male members of the congregation came to

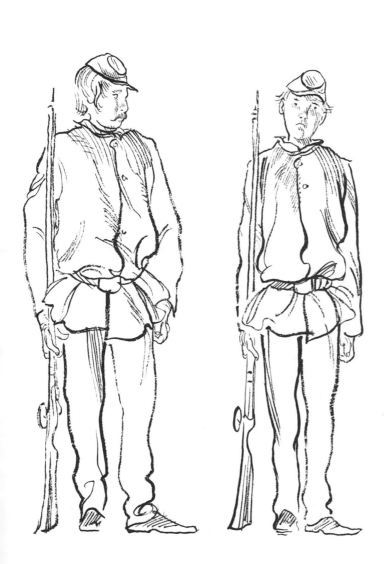

Jonathan and said that there were a number of young fellows who would like to form a militia company. The men thought it would be a good idea, as it would keep the boys out of mischief part of the time.

The next week, lawyer Walcott put a notice in the Litchfield *Enquirer* stating that the "Israel Putnam Guards" were in the process of formation, and that any able man between the ages of eighteen and fifty should report at the horse sheds of the Congregational Church on Thursday night. Forty from Litchfield signed up and twenty-five from surrounding towns.

On his next trip to New Haven for the session of the Connecticut legislature, Jonathan Walcott met with the governor, who gave him the proper forms for enrolling his company in the Connecticut State Militia, and his captain's commission, after Walcott had presented evidence that he and two other men had been unanimously elected captain, first lieutenant and second lieutenant, respectively, by the men of the company.

Next, Walcott dropped in on the captain of the New Haven company of the Governor's Foot Guards, who recommended a book on infantry tactics and another prepared by the Mattatuck Ancient Drum Band of Waterbury on regulation fife and drum calls. Nightly after supper Jonathan sat in front of his fireplace with a candlestick in one hand and the manual of arms in the other.

At the next meeting of the company, the choosing of a rifle was debated. Some were in favor of the Springfield .58 caliber, but others said the Springfield was too heavy and favored the Derringer .40. As a compromise, the British Enfield .50 was chosen, without the knowledge that no other militia company in the state used that caliber ammunition.

As soon as the snow was off the ground, the company had its first drill. Walcott, armed with his father's sword, soon found that some of the men had trouble with "Left, right, left, right." Then he remembered a suggestion given him by the captain of the Governor's Foot Guards. He tied a small bundle of hay to the left ankle and a bundle of straw to the right ankle of the men who could not tell their right foot from their left. Now the command was "Hay-foot, straw-foot, hay-foot, straw-foot." And the problem was solved.

On July 4, 1834, the Israel Putnam Guards, under the command of Captain Jonathan Walcott, made its first appearance on the Litchfield Common. The new uniforms had arrived and the Enfield rifles from England. The uniforms were a modest copy of those worn by the Governor's Foot Guards. Considering that the length of Litchfield's Main Street was the longest march the company had ever taken, the men put on a creditable appearance and kept in step most of the time. The townspeople were mightily impressed, and more than one man was heard to say, "I'll vouch that Jonathan Walcott is smarter than any of them West Pointers."

This remark was typical of the American distrust of the professional soldier, particularly if that soldier had graduated from the U.S. Military Academy. And this attitude prevailed during most of the Civil War in both North and South. It derived from the "Concord-Lexington legend"—a legend that was actually pure myth.

People believed that if untrained militiamen could whip disciplined British regulars, there was no reason on earth why good, clean-living American citizens needed West Pointers to tell them what to do on the battlefield. The Professionals were the ones who were defeated on April 19, 1775, when "the embattled farmers stood and fired the shot 'heard round the world.' "

The fallacy in this belief lay in the fact that the men on Lexington Common were not a company of militia. They were truly "embattled farmers" who had come out individually with their hunting rifles. If they'd been militiamen with a captain like fictional Jonathan Walcott who had bought a book to study military tactics, they would have fought by the book and been slaughtered.

The Americans at Lexington were guerrillas, then called "Minute Men." They used hunting rifles, not the heavy, inaccurate, smoothbore "Brown Bess" muskets of the British. They might fire an initial volley, but from then on it was "fire at will," and every man for himself. The Minute Man picked his target and stalked him as he would a deer. This was the kind of fighting which won the battle of Bennington for Ethan Allen's Green Mountain Boys. It was the untrained militia who lost battles for Washington until he obtained professional generals such as Von Steuben and Lafayette. But for seventy-five years, militia captains bristled when West Point was mentioned.

Jonathan Walcott's Israel Putnam Guards were better known to the Connecticut State Militia's adjutant general as Company H, Third Connecticut Volunteer Infantry. Jonathan had never seen the rest of his regiment, and so he looked forward to Muster Day with great anticipation. That would be his first experience as a regimental officer.

But now let us go to recorded history rather than fictionalized facts.

Simon Griffin of Nelson, New Hampshire, enlisted as a private in the Civil War in the state militia, and came out of the war a major general. In a speech delivered around 1880 he described a Muster Day of 1850.

"The regimental muster was the Red-letter-day of the whole year for men & boys, & even some girls. No one who ever tasted the delicious gingerbread of those days, made in sheets of about 5 x 8 in. of surface & an inch thick, light, sweet & spongy, will ever forget it. It was never found in its perfection except at those musters & when the law no longer required those parades, the recipes for making that gingerbread must have been lost. To that was added on muster days those pink & white sticks of candy, cider, pop, beer, raw oysters & other good things to eat & drink, & with side shows & other contrivances. To go to those musters, we used to start in the middle of the night, so as to be on the field before sunrise. And a very long & full day we made of it, and how we enjoyed the martial music.

"The law required that every enrolled soldier would appear on parade armed & equipped, & each was warned a certain number of days in advance by a written or printed notice from the officers of his company to appear at the musters with his musket in good condition, with ramrod & bayonet, knapsack, canteen & cartridge box, with two spare flints & a priming wire & brush. These last were for the old flintlocks.

"There would be company drills in the morning, in which each Light Infantry, Grenadier, Cavalry, Artillery, & Rifle Company was anxious to excel.

"Then came the battalion drill & the review of the regiment by the general, attended by a gorgeous staff, each of whom we believed to be the equal of a Field Marshal.

"And when the sun went down, with heads full of excitement & wonders of the day—& some of the older ones possibly with something stronger—we would start for home & the woods & the little murmuring streams as we passed along were all vocal with the strains of that martial music which had charmed our ears all the day long & in which our memories & imaginations still remained."

Gingerbread and murmuring streams! Such was the military education of the volunteer soldier who would do his postgraduate work at Bull Run, Antietam, Fredericksburg, Chancellorsville and Gettysburg.

CHAPTER FOUR

WE'RE COMING, FATHER ABRAHAM

THE reaction of the Northern press to President Lincoln's proclamation was not so unanimous as might be expected. Generally the New England newspapers were enthusiastic in their support of the President, but there was strong dissent as well. The Bangor (Maine) *Union* printed: "Democrats of Maine, the loyal sons of the South have gathered around Charleston as your fathers gathered around Boston. . . . Those who have inaugurated this unholy and unjustifiable war, are no friends of yours. Will you aid them in their work of subjugation and tyranny?"

The New York *Express* was even more vitriolic: "The South in self-preservation has been driven to the wall and forced to proclaim its independence. A servile insurrection and wholesale slaughter of the whites will alone satisfy the murderous designs of the Abolitionists. The Administration, egged on by the halloo of the Black Republican journals of this city, has sent its mercenary forces to pick a quarrel and initiate the work of desolation and ruin. . . ."

In the same vein, the Utica (New York) *Observer* said: "Of all the wars which have disgraced the human race, it has been reserved for our own enlightened nation to be involved in the most useless and foolish one. . . . Admit if you please, that they [Confederates] are rebels and traitors: they are beyond our reach. Why should we destroy ourselves in injuring them?"

Nevertheless, on the day Lincoln's proclamation was received in Harrisburg, Pennsylvania, one battalion of Pennsylvania militia came straggling into Washington before night.

The President's proclamation was backed up by telegrams to the governors from Secretary of War Simon Cameron. The regimental quotas were as follows: Maine 1, New Hampshire 1, Vermont 1, Massachusetts 2, Rhode Island 1, Connecticut 1, New York 17, New Jersey 4, Pennsylvania 16, Delaware 1, Tennessee 2, Maryland 4, Virginia 3, North Carolina 2, Kentucky 4, Arkansas 1, Missouri 4, Ohio 13, Indiana 6, Illinois 6, Michigan 1, Iowa 1, Minnesota 1 and Wisconsin 1.

As was expected, the governors of Virginia, North Carolina and Arkansas refused to send troops, since those states were in the process of secession. The border states, Kentucky, Tennessee, and Maryland, likewise refused. The other states had to organize their regiments and equip them before they could send them to Washington.

Massachusetts was the only Northern state to be fully prepared for the emergency. The Land of the Bean and the Cod has always been proud of its Minute Man tradition: the rugged individualist who was always prepared, who left his plow and oxen in the field, grabbed his flintlock from above the fireplace and was at Bunker Hill in no time flat.

In December 1860, less than a month after Lincoln's election, Adjutant-general Schouler of the Massachusetts State Militia sent a recommendation to

Governor Nathaniel Banks that the State Militia should be expanded, that incomplete companies should be filled and that the names and addresses of all militiamen should be on file in the state Capitol. By January 16, 1861, the Massachusetts State Militia was on a full alert, although no such recommendation had come from the War Department.

When Lincoln's proclamation was received over the telegraph by Massachusetts Governor John Andrew, four regiments were ready to "take the cars." These regiments were not run-of-the-mill "Muster Day Militia." For months the companies had held weekly drills, with target practice, close formation drill and lectures on army regulations. The Massachusetts legislature had equipped them with tents, company kitchens, stout boots, new rifles and rugged woolen uniforms to replace the Fourth of July regalia.

Of the four regiments available for immediate action, Governor Andrew, upon receipt of his quota, chose the Sixth and Eighth Massachusetts Volunteer Infantry. The two regiments were ordered to muster immediately on Boston Common.

At 11:00 A.M. on April 17, the Sixth Massachusetts marched to the State House in Boston and received its new regimental colors from Governor Andrew. At 7:00 P.M., it "took the cars" for New York. At Worcester and Springfield, the fire departments threw up streams of water as the train passed. In New York the next day, the officers were invited to breakfast at the Astor House. The regiment reached Philadelphia at seven that night.

On the morning of April 19, the anniversary of the battles of Concord and Lexington, the Sixth Massachusetts reached Baltimore. The night before, the president of the Wilmington & Philadelphia Railroad had warned Colonel Jones of the Sixth that his passage through Baltimore might be challenged by a mob. Just before reaching Baltimore, Colonel Jones went through each coach and gave this order:

"The regiment will march through Baltimore in columns of sections, arms

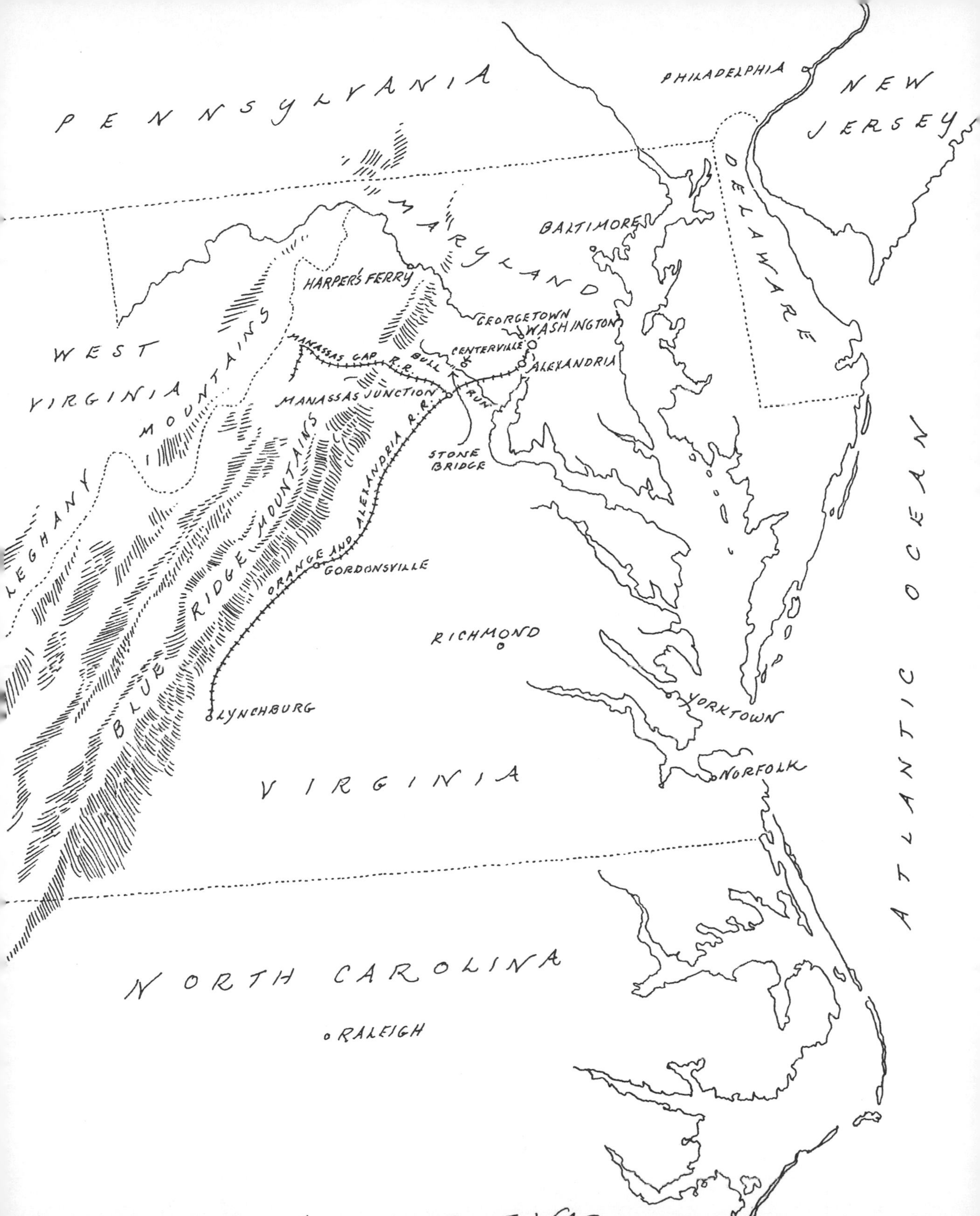

PENNSYLVANIA

PHILADELPHIA

NEW JERSEY

DELAWARE

MARYLAND

BALTIMORE

HARPER'S FERRY

WEST VIRGINIA

ALLEGHANY MOUNTAINS

MANASSAS GAP R.R.

GEORGETOWN

WASHINGTON

CENTERVILLE

BULL RUN

ALEXANDRIA

MANASSAS JUNCTION

ORANGE AND ALEXANDRIA R.R.

STONE BRIDGE

BLUE RIDGE MOUNTAINS

GORDONSVILLE

RICHMOND

YORKTOWN

LYNCHBURG

NORFOLK

VIRGINIA

ATLANTIC OCEAN

NORTH CAROLINA

o RALEIGH

.. EASTERN THEATER OF WAR ..

at will. You will undoubtedly be insulted, abused and perhaps assaulted, to which you must pay no attention whatsoever, but march with your faces square to the front, and pay no attention to the mob even if they throw stones, bricks or other missiles; but if you are fired upon, and any of you are hit, your officers will order you to fire. Do not fire into any promiscuous crowds, but select any man you may see aiming at you, and be sure you drop him."

In those days, railroad corporations were relatively small. With no coordination between the roads, it was necessary for a traveler to change trains every hundred miles or less. In this case, the Wilmington & Philadelphia did not connect with the Baltimore & Ohio which would take the Sixth to Washington. Coaches going from Philadelphia to Washington were detached and drawn by horses two miles through the streets of Baltimore to the B&O station. To lighten the coaches, Colonel Jones had ordered the Sixth to detrain and march the two miles. Each soldier was issued twenty rounds of ammunition.

The streets were lined with supporters of the Confederacy, men and women wearing Rebel rosettes on their coat lapels or hats. There were boos and cat-calls, but no violence up to this point. Suddenly gangs burst through the crowd, a few rocks were thrown, followed by a shower of paving blocks. Men of the Sixth were going down, some with serious head injuries. Then someone fired a pistol, and a private fell dead.

The regiment halted, and a company fired into the crowd. Several civilians were killed, and the crowd panicked. The governor of Maryland sent a telegram to President Lincoln pleading that no more troops be sent through Baltimore until emotions had cooled, and James Carroll penned his patriotic lines to the tune of the innocent Christmas carol "Oh Christmas Tree":

> The despot's heel is on thy shore,
> Maryland, my Maryland.
> His torch is at thy temple door,

WE'RE COMING, FATHER ABRAHAM
Maryland, my Maryland.
Avenge the patriotic gore,
That flecked the streets of Baltimore,
And be the battle queen of yore,
Maryland, my Maryland.

The Sixth Massachusetts received an exuberant welcome when it reached Washington. It was billeted in the House of Representatives since Congress was not then in session. The basement of the Capitol was also used. Ovens had been installed to bake bread. But the cheering populace fell silent when it was realized that except for one full regiment of infantry and a few poorly trained companies of District of Columbia militia, Washington was defenseless and completely isolated from the rest of the nation. President Lincoln had acceded to the plea of the governor of Maryland and additional troops had not been sent through Baltimore to avoid bloodshed. But even if he had not agreed, the situation would have been the same. Crowds of hoodlums had burned railroad bridges and cut telegraph lines. The President could not communicate with the states. The War Department had no way of knowing how many troops were on the way, and so preparations could not be made to receive them.

With Virginia now on a wartime footing, and the resignation from the U.S. Army of Colonel Robert E. Lee to become major general of the Virginia State Militia, Secretary of War Cameron saw the Army and Washington itself threatened by a dangerous situation at Harper's Ferry, Virginia. If the Virginia Militia were to take Harper's Ferry, it would have the Arsenal with its large stock of rifles that were so badly needed for the poorly armed militia regiments Cameron hoped were on their way.

Moreover, if the Rebels could cross the Potomac at Harper's Ferry and sweep down the north bank of the river, Washington could be taken from the north or west. Coming through Maryland, they would be supported by most of the residents and even if the Confederates were unable to capture Washington, they could cut off its roads and food supply.

General Scott poohpoohed this reasoning. While he admitted that Harper's Ferry was defenseless, he argued that by burning the highway and railroad bridges the Rebels could be prevented from crossing the Potomac by a small detachment which could be rushed there over a branch of the Baltimore & Ohio railroad that ran from Relay Station between Baltimore and Washington to Winchester, Virginia.

Scott was convinced that time was on his side. Lee's troops would have a long way to travel to Harper's Ferry. They would have to come from Richmond to Manassas Junction, transfer to the little Manassas Gap Railroad to reach the Shenandoah Valley and then march down the Valley to Harper's Ferry. (Railroads played a crucial part in the Battle of Bull Run, and they would become increasingly important throughout the war.)

Scott's main concern was Washington. He reasoned that Beauregard would have no trouble in mobilizing his army, for the South was laced with railroads with troop transport as their chief priority. On the other hand, Scott could not be sure that the Union state militia regiments would be able to reach Washington. Suppose Maryland refused to let them pass through the state even if they avoided Baltimore. If the militia regiments fought their way through, they would immediately drive Maryland into the Confederacy, and while they were fighting, Washington could be taken without firing a shot.

Actually, General-in-Chief Winfield Scott was in no condition to command an army. Born in 1786, he was now seventy-five years old. In 1814 he had been commissioned major general for his bravery at the Battle of Lundy's Lane during the War of 1812. In 1841 he had been made general-in-chief of the U.S. Army. George Washington had been the only other officer to hold that rank. In the Mexican War, Scott had captured Mexico City. Now the general suffered severely from gout. He could scarcely walk, and every step caused him extreme

General Winfield Scott

General P. G. T. Beauregard

pain. He moved from his house to an apartment nearer the War Department and when he drove to the White House, President Lincoln would come down to the carriage to spare the old general the pain of getting out and climbing the long staircase to the President's office.

Business was at a standstill in the capital. With the inability to get supplies through Maryland, many stores had closed, and the price of a barrel of flour had risen to fifteen dollars. The government had taken over all the salt meat in preparation for the arrival of an army.

Now came more bad news. The Norfolk Navy Yard had been captured along with Harper's Ferry! With the secessionist disorders in Maryland, the noose seemed to be tightening around the District of Columbia. General Scott presented Lincoln with his plan for the defense of the capital. It centered on Executive Square, containing the White House and the Treasury. If the White House could not be held, the Treasury would be the final stronghold. It had its own water supply, and Scott put 2,000 barrels of flour in the basement.

But there was a sudden, unexpected ray of hope. Without a word in advance, since the telegraph wires were cut, the Eighth Massachusetts Infantry and the silk-stocking New York Seventh marched into Washington. And how they got there makes an exciting tale.

The Sixth and Eighth Massachusetts Regiments had been mustered into service at the same time after Lincoln's proclamation. They were lumped under the command of a militia brigadier general, Benjamin F. Butler. He was a sharp, some said disreputable, lawyer from Lowell. He was short, partly bald, carried a little pot belly and wore a villainous mustache. Later in the war, he was variously known as "Old Cockeye," "Beast Butler," and "Bottled Up Butler." The first nickname came from the fact that one of his eyes stared off to the side while the other looked straight ahead. Other lawyers said that Butler's success in court was due to the fact that he could watch a witness and be foreman of the jury at the same time.

44

When the Sixth Massachusetts left for Washington via Baltimore, Butler remained behind with the Eighth, because not all of its supplies had arrived. On the morning of April 18, the regiment was outfitted, almost, and that afternoon, with General Butler leading the column, it marched up the hill to the State House where there was a speech by Governor Andrew. What the Governor could not see behind the closed, compact ranks was a team of tailors sewing the required two brass buttons on the back of each soldier's coat. The Eighth left for Washington without hearing about the earlier fate of the Sixth in Baltimore.

When Butler and his men reached Philadelphia, S. M. Felton, president of the Philadelphia, Wilmington & Baltimore Railroad, called to see the general. Felton announced that his line would no longer transport troops through Baltimore, that even if it wanted to, it could not, because the secessionists had burned several bridges.

Butler was under order to go through Baltimore, but that was now obviously impossible. He tried to reach General Scott, but the telegraph wires were still down. There was only one other way to reach Washington without too much delay: that was to go to Annapolis, below Baltimore, if transportation could be found. Felton said that he could carry the regiment to the north bank of the Susquehanna in Maryland, and that, if it had not been seized by the secessionists, there was a ferryboat large enough to ship the regiment to Annapolis. Butler believed he would be attacked there, but he was confident that with the cadets of the Naval Academy, he could hold off any mob. Furthermore, other regiments would have to use Annapolis and he would soon be reinforced.

Felton delivered the Eighth Regiment to Perryville without incident. Although the trip from Annapolis to Washington is not of historic importance, some of the emergencies encountered highlight an important Union asset—comparable perhaps to its superiority in manpower over sources of supply. This was Yankee ingenuity—having the know-how to cope with problems requiring mechanical skills. This ability to repair, rebuild, and improve equipment

mitigated to a large extent the effect of the professionally trained Confederate generals and a better-commanded Rebel Army.

Northern soldiers were mechanics, farmers, fishermen, whaling men, carpenters, and plumbers. The farmer had to know how to repair his equipment. The carpenter, who should have been in the Engineer Corps, was carrying a rifle, but he still knew how to build a barrack or a snug shelter while in winter quarters. The Southern infantryman, who had little farm equipment, was helpless when faced with problems beyond using his rifle.

When Butler and his regiment arrived at Annapolis, it was dark. The ferryboat was no more than anchored when a skiff with five Naval Academy cadets came alongside. Admitted on board under guard, they said that they had been sent by their commanding officer who feared that the ferryboat carried a party of thugs whose purpose might be to seize or destroy the U.S.S. *Constitution* ("Old Ironsides") which was tied up at the Academy. Finding a Union regiment aboard, they pleaded with Butler to save the *Constitution.* Butler, who did not know that "Old Ironsides" was at the Academy, thought they were referring to the Constitution of the United States and snapped, "That's what we're here for."

The cadets set the general right and told him that there were not enough cadets left at the Academy to move the *Constitution* to a safe mooring. To Butler this was not a problem. He called up Company D, composed entirely of deep-sea fishermen from Marblehead. The *Constitution* was manned and soon anchored away from shore.

A day after Butler's Eighth Massachusetts arrived in Annapolis, the steamer *Boston* came in with the New York Seventh Regiment. The Seventh was New York's society regiment. In its ranks as privates were men who owned banks, insurance companies, railroads and brokerage houses. Its uniforms were elegant, its band one of the finest, and on muster days the gourmet food was provided by Delmonico's restaurant. When the Seventh landed, from its baggage wagons came velvet-covered camp stools, silverware, the best of china and picnic hampers packed by Delmonico's. The Seventh had answered Lincoln's call and was now off on what they believed would be a three-month outing.

Butler's orders were to proceed to Washington immediately, but there were no railroad cars at Annapolis. They had all been removed. In addition to this problem, he now had the New York Seventh as an additional responsibility. Although Butler, a Massachusetts Militia brigadier general, had no jurisdiction over New York troops, the colonel of the Seventh was more than willing to recognize Butler's rank and let him feed and transport the Seventh Regiment.

Butler ordered his men to take possession of the railroad station. In a building which the stationmaster had said was empty, they found a small steam lomomotive which had been as thoroughly dismantled as unskilled hands could accomplish. Butler turned to the two companies in charge of the station and asked if there were any men present who knew anything about an engine such as this. Private Charles Homans of Company E stepped forward and said, "That engine was built in our shop. My initials are chiseled on the under side of the boiler." Soon the locomotive was in running order.

But now Butler's advance guard sent back word that most of the railroad tracks between Annapolis and Relay Station were torn up. So the Massachusetts Eighth and the New York Seventh made the march from Annapolis to Washington. It took them two days. This was not bad for militia regiments that had never marched even two miles in one day. In fact it was a far better record than the march from Washington to Bull Run in mid-July 1861.

CHAPTER FIVE

FOCUS ON WASHINGTON

WASHINGTON was jubilant over the arrival of Butler's troops. Throngs of women came to the Capitol where they were billeted. General Scott was greatly relieved. He felt that with better than 3,000 men on hand Washington could be held, at least temporarily. President Lincoln reviewed the new troops as they marched past the White House.

The next day, another Massachusetts regiment arrived, along with the First Rhode Island Infantry. The ladies of Washington were thrilled by the daily parades and drills. The old town was a gay city again.

The First Rhode Island was commanded by Colonel Ambrose E. Burnside. He was a West Point graduate, a successful businessman, and an inveterate gambler. The latter pastime had nearly cost him his commission at West Point. He wore magnificent side whiskers, a style which was given his name in reverse. William Sprague, Governor of Rhode Island, an attractive young man said to be the richest man in the state, had come along to see the fun. Soon

General Ambrose Everett Burnside

Sprague was constantly seen in the company of Kate Chase, daughter of Treasury Secretary Salmon P. Chase. Kate was the most beautiful woman in Washington and the affair was the talk of the town.

By the middle of May the ban on travel through Baltimore was lifted, the regiments began pouring in and the government's problems became herculean. The food which the Quartermaster General had stored was soon exhausted, and fresh supplies were not coming in fast enough. The Ordnance Department was in trouble. Many of the regiments were coming into the city unarmed. The surplus rifles at the Springfield Armory were distributed but additional arms were hard to get now that the Harper's Ferry Arsenal was in the hands of the Rebels. Enfield rifles were ordered from Great Britain and contracts were made to convert old Mexican War flintlocks to percussion fire.

But almost as serious as the lack of rifles was the problem of those regiments which *were* armed. In some states militia regiments had selected their own weapons, and their rifles had a wide range of calibers. Therefore the standard U.S. Army ammunition, which was .58 caliber, would not fit all of them. Under such conditions, a regiment running out of ammunition on the battlefield might not be able to borrow from a neighboring regiment.

Less serious, but still a problem, were the uniforms. State militia regiments, and even companies, chose their own uniforms. Their colors encompassed the rainbow. Their styles ranged from the colonial militia, Napoleon's Grande Armée, and Moroccan Zouaves to the Italian Carabinieri. There was a serious predicament: gray was a favorite color with the militia on both sides. On the battlefield, who would be shooting whom?

The outfit which was by far the most colorful among the new arrivals was the New York Fire Zouaves. Colonel Elmer Ellsworth, a Regular Army officer who felt that his career was being stifled by the War Department, obtained permission to go to New York and recruit a regiment from the city's volunteer fire companies. He had put together nearly a thousand of New

Zouave

York's toughest plug-uglies and trained them superbly. They soon became famous for their intricate exhibition drills. But what made them outstanding in any parade was the Zouave uniform copied from the troops of what was then French Morocco. It was composed of long, red, baggy pantaloons (Turkish style), brown leather leggings, a short blue jacket (later to be known as Eisenhower style) trimmed with red braid, and a red fez with a black tassel (like a Shriner's).

When Ellsworth's Fire Zouaves arrived in the city, Washington was entranced. The people had never seen anything like the precision drills which were staged daily by the Zouaves. But soon the city was wondering whether the whole Confederate Army would be any more disruptive. The Zouaves had taken over Washington. When on parade, Ellsworth's discipline was iron-clad, but as soon as the men were dismissed, they went wild.

Zouaves playfully pushed each other through the plate-glass windows of stores. Any stray pig, and there were plenty of them in the Washington streets, was slaughtered and barbecued on the spot. When the Zouaves entered a saloon, it was a wreck when they left. One of their favorite entertainments was to march into a swank restaurant, run up a huge bill and then tell the proprietor to send it to Jefferson Davis.

But the role of the Fire Zouaves was not all destructive. When a fire bell rang, they leaped to action with wild wahoos. They usually managed to beat the not-so-rapid Washington volunteer firemen to the engine houses. At the foreman's cry of "Start her lively, boys," they dragged out the hand engines and raced at breakneck speed to the fire. Some critics accused them of starting fires so they could have the fun of putting them out.

In their fire fighting the New York Zouaves were as spectacular as in their drills. Disdaining ladders, they went up the sides of buildings by climbing from one window ledge to another. Another method of ascent was to run out a line of hose, toss and hook the nozzle into the chimney, and go up the hose, hand over hand. When the fire was out they slid down the hose to the street.

Washington, which a month before had been pleading for troops to defend it and then had been entranced by the colorfulness of the dress parades, now wondered if it could survive the summer. A serious health menace had developed with which the city was unable to cope.

Washington had always been an unhealthy city, especially in the summer. The city was dirty; even Pennsylvania Avenue was as yet unpaved. Garbage was thrown into the streets for the stray pigs to eat. Where the Mall now runs from the Lincoln Memorial to the Washington Monument, there was a canal which was nothing more than an open sewer where dead animals floated in the steaming summer sun. Its obnoxious fumes infiltrated the downtown area. There were annual typhoid epidemics due to impure water. Added to these problems was the presence of some 30,000 untrained troops, most of whom had never been away from home or even camped out overnight.

Few militia colonels knew the proper method of laying out an encampment and the tents were placed too close together. They knew nothing about locating or constructing latrines, or "sinks," as they were then called. Army regulations prescribed the distance that sinks should be dug from the hospital tents or the regimental kitchen, but few of the militia colonels had read the regulations. Many had no sinks dug, and the men "went" where they pleased. Dysentery and measles spread like a forest fire among the troops and then infected the civilian population. There was not a military hospital in the city, and many regiments did not have hospital tents. Regimental surgeons were often uneducated country doctors or just plain quacks.

In those early days of national mobilization, there were also the men who became ill by just not living right. Some who had never seen the city's bright lights soon contracted venereal diseases from the thriving brothels of Washing-

ton. The underage drummer boy whose mother had rigidly insisted on his Saturday night bath didn't have to take one now, and he could change his underwear when he felt like it. Soon the army was infested with lice, and off-duty hours were spent picking them out of underwear. There were those who would have liked to bathe regularly, but could get no water. Some regimental camps in Washington and Georgetown, then a separate city, were so far away from a water supply that there was only enough for drinking and cooking.

The farm boy was used to the winter diet of salt pork and salt beef, but regiments such as the affluent New York Seventh "wouldn't touch the stuff." And now we meet a Civil War phenomenon, the army sutler. Army regulations provided that in an encampment, the officers might appoint and license a civilian sutler who could set up a store in a shack or tent and sell to the men articles which the army did not stock. Prices were fixed by the sutler, but part of the profits went to the "regimental fund." Soldiers such as those of the New York Seventh shunned the mess tent and patronized the sutler, who provided them with food which doubtless tasted better than salt beef but which was poorly prepared and unwholesome. Soldiers who lived off the sutler frequently became ill.

All during this period, the Army (which was now only a conglomerate of militia regiments, with a few battalions of regulars), was suffering from the incapacity and senility of General Scott. His military attitudes were still those of 1812 and the Mexican War. In the presence of Scott and President Lincoln on the White House lawn, Thaddeus S. C. Lowe had demonstrated the use of a balloon for military observation. Lowe went up to a height where he could see Confederate movements as far as Fairfax Court House, Virginia. This was the first time that anyone in Washington knew where Confederate troops were. Lincoln was favorably impressed, but Scott would have nothing to do with balloons. (By 1862 they were being used extensively and profitably by General

McClellan in his Peninsular campaign.) General Scott stubbornly opposed field maneuvers of even a brigade, and he specifically prohibited division maneuvers on the ground that they would only be a vain show.

At this point, General Beauregard's army around Manassas Junction, Virginia, was also badly organized, so that Scott, with little opposition, could have occupied enough Virginia territory to have held field maneuvers with artillery support and sham battles with blank ammunition. Instead, only company and regimental drills were held in the streets and squares of Washington and Georgetown. And the citizens were wishing that the bands would learn to play something besides "Columbia, the Gem of the Ocean" and "Rally 'Round the Flag, Boys."

CHAPTER SIX

ARMS AND THE MAN

TO visualize the actions in a war which began over a hundred years ago, it will be helpful to know the organization of the armies. In 1861, how many men were in a corps, a regiment, a brigade, and a division? How many guns formed an artillery battery?

Next, it will be helpful to have some familiarity with the weapons of the Civil War. What were they and where did they come from? How accurate was the muzzle-loading Springfield rifle? What was the effective range of the 12-pounder cannon, and how was the cavalry equipped?

These questions and a few others will be answered in this chapter, particularly as they relate to the Battle of Bull Run. The breech-loading carbines which the cavalry used later in the war, the observation balloons and the field telegraph will not be discussed, but only those army units and weapons of war that were on the field Sunday morning, July 21, 1861.

The organization of the Union and Confederate armies was virtually the same. The high-ranking officers of both armies were West Point graduates and adhered to the U.S. Army Regulations upon which they had been nurtured. The basic unit was the company, which, at full strength, numbered 100 men, including two musicians who were assigned to the regimental band. A captain and two lieutenants commanded a company. Ten companies comprised a regiment, a colonel commanding, with a band of twenty. Before Bull Run, affluent regiments enlisted additional musicians, paid from the "mess fund," but all regimental bands were sent home in August of 1861 as an unessential drain on manpower and generally useless in a tough campaign. The only remaining bands during the rest of the war were brigade bands stationed at permanent bases.

From the regiment upward, larger army units were multiples of three. Three regiments composed a brigade (3,000) under a brigadier general. Three brigades (9,000) formed a division, commanded by a major general, and three divisions, under a major general, the highest army rank at the time, formed an army corps. According to regulations, three corps formed an army, if under a single command, but this was conditioned by circumstances of terrain, objective and the strength of the enemy. The commander of such an army as Lee's Army of Northern Virginia, Sherman's Army of the Tennessee and McClellan's Army of the Potomac was responsible to the Secretary of War or the Chief of Staff if there was one. Two exceptions were at Bull Run, when Winfield Scott was still General-in-Chief, and after Gettysburg, when Grant held the same commission.

To those who wish to do further reading on the War Between the States and who follow this author's guide to the number of men on the battlefield after the disastrous defeat of the Union Army at Fredericksburg (December 13, 1862) and Lee's rout at Gettysburg (July 3, 1863), a word of caution is in order.

The fifth New Hampshire Infantry went into Fredericksburg with nearly a

General J. E. B. Stuart

General Philip Henry Sheridan

General Robert E. Lee

full complement of 1,000 men. Like many other Union regiments on that bloody day, it came out with a handful, a completely shattered unit. In such cases, it was the practice of the U.S. Army to retire the regiment temporarily until the colonel or some regimental officer could go back to his home state and recruit enough men to fill the ranks. Then the regiment went back into action.

Under the Confederate War Department, decimated regiments were kept in service, and new regiments were recruited. Thus an account of a battle might state that Confederate General Longstreet had three divisions in his corps, while facing Hooker with one. Actually Longstreet may have had no more than 4,000 men while Hooker had 9,000. This was especially true after Gettysburg, when the entire Army of Northern Virginia could count little more than 30,000 men.

In addition to the line officers who commanded the units we have listed, there were other staff officers and even civilians whose duties were to keep the units functioning. In charge of regimental supplies was the quartermaster. He usually held the noncommissioned rank of sergeant. He procured food for the men, forage for the horses, uniforms, blankets, harnesses, tents, etc. He was directly responsible to the colonel of the regiment.

The adjutant, usually a lieutenant, kept the regimental records, copied the colonel's orders for distribution to the company commanders, conducted the colonel's communications with brigade headquarters and kept the casualty lists.

The regimental surgeon, a captain, was usually the only medical man in the unit. His orderlies were privates drawn from the ranks. He was always overtaxed in time of action and confined himself to doling out pills when the regiment was in camp. Many regimental surgeons had never seen a medical school. All their medical education had been drawn from books. They knew little or nothing about the use of antiseptics or the treatment of infections. Consequently, a bullet wound in the arm or leg often resulted in amputation.

The regimental chaplain had the privileges and pay of a commissioned officer, but without his rank. In the Regular Army, he was assigned by the War Department, but in the militia regiments, he had been elected, along with the other officers, before the regiment left home. The chaplain was chosen according to the predominant religious faith of the regiment. The chaplains for the Louisiana Tigers and New York's Fighting Sixty-ninth were Roman Catholic priests, while most chaplains of New England regiments were Congregational or Unitarian ministers.

In addition to conducting the Sunday morning service or mass, the chaplain visited the sick and wounded in the hospital tent and wrote letters home for those who were illiterate or too disabled to write. He wrote chiding letters to wives who rarely wrote to their husbands. He wrote letters of consolation to widows after they had been notified of their loss by the War Deparment, and he conducted military funerals. Not as a duty, but as a service to history, the chaplain usually kept a diary of the regiment's activities. Thus, most of the regimental histories of the Civil War in existence today were written from the notes in these journals.

An important adjunct to the regiment was the wagon master. Transportation was a serious problem in the early days of the war, and partially responsible for the agonizingly slow march of General Irvin McDowell's army down the Warrenton Turnpike to Bull Run. At that time a regiment was allowed ten wagons. Later this was reduced to six, but many militia regiments arrived in Washington with as many as fifty. Even the privates had brought so many things from home that they couldn't carry them on their backs. Later the contents of the wagons were limited to tents, ammunition, cooking equipment, food, spare clothing, medical supplies and the officers' luggage. The wagon master supervised the loading and unloading of the wagon train, the care of the mules or horses, and the routing and timing of the wagon train while on the march.

And finally, a few more words about the sutler, who was alternately cursed and cheered by the troops. He was sometimes called the "Quartermaster Extraordinary" for in 1861, the Army made no provision for supplying the troops with tobacco, sweets, sewing kits, postcards and the little extras which make a soldier's life brighter or easier. The Post Exchange was unheard of and the sutler filled this need also. But the other side of the coin was his consistent practice of gouging the men, charging exorbitant prices for everything. The sutler purchased all of his supplies through the Army Commissary Department, but he was free to charge what he pleased. He could sell anything the troops needed or thought they needed, except liquor. Those who violated this prohibition always ran the risk that, during the night, the corporal of the guard might make off with the whole supply. The common soldier, who was paid thirteen dollars a month, looked upon the sutler as a coward who was getting rich while the soldier risked his life. But the sutler got rich only from "society" regiments, such as the New York Seventh and the Washington Artillery of New Orleans, whose men did not depend on their army pay for spending money.

The South, which was soon to depend for arms on running British Enfield rifles through the blockade, was adequately supplied with shoulder weapons in the spring of 1861. As mentioned earlier, during the spring and summer of 1860, Buchanan's Secretary of War, John B. Floyd, a secessionist, shipped 135,000 rifles from the Springfield Armory and the Harper's Ferry Arsenal to federal arsenals and forts in the South where they could be seized by the Confederates after the secession of the Southern states. So obvious was Secretary Floyd's purpose in transferring these weapons that the Mobile

Advertiser editorialized: "We are much obliged to Secretary Floyd for the foresight he has displayed in disarming the North and arming the South in this emergency." And this occurred even before Lincoln had been elected.

This transfer did not immediately embarrass the U.S. Army, which numbered only 12,000 before the bombardment of Fort Sumter. At that time too there were still 20,000 rifles and smoothbore muskets at Harper's Ferry. Most of these had been converted from flintlock to percussion cap. But obviously the store of arms was insufficient when Lincoln called for 75,000 volunteers in April of 1861 and 200,000 more in May.

The 20,000 shoulder weapons at Harper's Ferry were lost when Virginia troops seized the Arsenal and its machinery. However, the results of this raid were disappointing to the Confederacy. Due to inefficiency and a lack of skilled labor, the Richmond Arsenal was able to turn out only 2,000 rifles a month against the 5,000 produced in the same period with the same machinery at the Harper's Ferry Arsenal.

At Springfield, Massachusetts the basic infantry weapon of the U.S. Army during the Civil War, the Springfield rifle, was manufactured. The Springfield was simple to operate and sturdy enough to stand up under a drubbing on the battlefield. Its spare parts were easily applied. It had only fifteen parts, including screws. Its length was 49.3 inches, its weight just under ten pounds and its caliber .58. The cartridge for the Springfield contained 60 grains of black powder and its muzzle velocity was about 600 feet per second.

The cartridge for both the Springfield and the British Enfield was of heavy paper with a thread tied around it just back of the ball. At the base of the cartridge was a tab similar to those used in opening cigarette packages. In loading, the infantryman tore off the tab with his teeth and poured the powder into the barrel. Again with his teeth he tore off all the paper except that tied to the ball. This remaining paper acted as wadding. Then he placed the paper-wrapped ball in the barrel and rammed it down with his ramrod. Next he drew the hammer back to half-cock and placed the cap on the nipple under it. Finally he drew the hammer back to full-cock and was ready to fire. It took a trained soldier about thirty seconds to load and fire. The cap was a small copper thimble, resembling a sawed-off .22 rifle shell, containing fulminate of mercury and powder.

The Springfield was practically foolproof, but its owner was not always so dependable. Too frequently, a soldier would load, then, confused by excitement, fear or the din of battle, would think he had fired and ram home another charge. This caused the weapon either to explode in its owner's face or to jam hopelessly. This sort of thing was quite common; one Springfield was found on the field of Gettysburg, the day after the battle, with ten charges in its barrel. The British Enfield was the back-up weapon of the North and the only hope for the South, because it was also .58 caliber and operated on the same principle as the Springfield.

Immediately after the bombardment of Sumter, Secretary of War Cameron, fearing that the Springfield Armory might not be able to keep up with the demand for rifles, ordered 200,000 Enfields from Britain and began letting out contracts to private manufacturers for duplicating the Springfield. The Samuel Colt Company of Hartford, Connecticut, makers of the legendary Colt revolver, made Springfields, as did the Derringer Company, which manufactured the pistol that was used to kill Lincoln. The Amoskeague Manufacturing Company of Manchester, New Hampshire, temporarily ceased producing steam fire engines and railroad locomotives and also turned to Springfields.

One of the ironies of the armament crisis was that breech-loading weapons had been made in the United States for fifteen years before Bull Run. The Sharps cavalry carbine, which a Johnny Reb later said could be loaded on Sunday and fired all week, was manufactured in Hartford, Connecticut. In

1850, the entire output had been sold to the British Army. Later in the Civil War, the British sold their supply of Sharps carbines back to the United States.

After the capture and dismantling of the Harper's Ferry Arsenal, the immediate problem of the Confederacy was not rifles, but ammunition. As any chemistry student knows, gunpowder is a mixture of saltpeter, charcoal and sulfur. It was some time after secession before a saltpeter supply was found. Everybody knew how to make charcoal and there were sulfur mines in Louisiana. But again, the lack of skilled labor in a primarily agricultural economy prevented mass production of rifle cartridges. When Beauregard arrived at Manassas Junction, he found the troops making their own ammunition. They cast their bullets with the bullet mold of the Revolution, poured the powder into cartridges made from newspapers and bound the bullet with thread they had brought to mend their clothes. Percussion caps were also in short supply because of a lack of copper and fulminate of mercury.

Except for some spectacular exploits of J.E.B. (Jeb) Stuart, Lee's chief of cavalry, and General Philip Henry Sheridan under Grant, cavalry was seldom used in battle during the Civil War. The terrain in most of Virginia and Tennessee did not lend itself to sweeping cavalry flanking movements, the classic use of cavalry in Europe. In only one battle of note between 1861 and 1865 was cavalry pitched against cavalry, and that was between troops of Stuart and Sheridan. Cavalry was used chiefly for reconnoitering the enemy, raids, sabotage and communications.

For equipment, the cavalryman, North or South, of course had his horse, usually of a sturdy breed. Next he had his saber. The saber's blade was curved and thirty-six inches long. With the metal hilt, the arm measured forty-two inches. The saber was seldom used except for broiling chickens as there was little hand-to-hand fighting.

More important to the cavalryman was his revolver, and his favorite was

General William T. Sherman

the Colt .44. Like the Springfield rifle, the Colt was so greatly in demand that it was made, under license from the Colt Firearms Company, in several different factories. The Confederacy converted one factory to make Colts, but without benefit of a license.

The virtues of the Colt revolver rested in its rapid fire, accuracy, balance, graceful design and simplicity in cleaning. The barrel was eight inches and the overall length was 13½ inches. A unique feature of the weapon was its swivel rammer, an integral part of the gun. The paper cartridge could not be used in the Colt, since the charges were placed in the six chambers of the cylinder and not through the barrel. The forward part of the rammer was a steel rod which clipped to the end of the barrel when not in use. This rod was jointed to a steel piston which fitted the chambers and which reached them through a casing under the butt of the barrel.

In loading, the cavalryman poured the requisite amount of powder into each chamber from a small powder horn, usually made of leather. Then he inserted the bullet. During this operation, the revolver was at half-cock, and the cylinder could be revolved with one finger. Now he unsnapped the rammer and swung down the handle. This caused a cogged semi-wheel to shove the piston into the chambers, one by one. Next, the chambers were capped and the hammer was brought to full cock. The rear sight was a notch in the hammer.

To clean the weapon, it was only necessary to knock out a steel wedge under the rear of the barrel. The barrel could then be removed as well as the cylinder. Sounds complicated? It was. But after firing six rounds, the cavalryman, if necessary, could gallop off and reload at leisure.

The third weapon of the 1861 cavalryman was the carbine. Within a few months after Bull Run, all Union carbines were to be breech-loading. By 1863 breech-loading rifles were also available, but the generals refused to change. Well after the Civil War, when surplus Springfields were being converted to breech-loaders, General Sherman wrote in his memoirs that the new or converted rifles would only cause men to waste ammunition.

The carbine in use at the outbreak of the war was called the "John Brown" carbine, because the objective of John Brown's raid on the Harper's Ferry Arsenal in 1859 was a supply of these carbines. Later, when the Virginia militia captured the Arsenal and its stock, the John Brown carbine also became the weapon of the Confederate cavalry. The barrel of this carbine was twenty-two inches and the caliber .52. The cavalryman carried his carbine in a leather socket attached to his saddle.

The Battle of Bull Run saw the first use of a new artillery weapon invented by Robert Parker Parrott, a native of Lee, New Hampshire. Born in 1804, Parrott graduated from West Point, became a mathematics professor there and in 1836 was placed in charge of the West Point cannon foundry.

Until the spring of 1861, the favorite artillery piece of the U.S. Army had been the bronze Napoleon cannon, both six- and twelve-pounders. The Napoleon was a simple, rugged gun. Its smoothbore handled solid shot adequately and had done so since the days of its namesake. It was ideal for firing cannister (an oversize shotgun shell), since it had no rifling to be damaged. It remained the favorite of many artillery units throughout the war and is the cannon most frequently shown in paintings and photographs of the war.

But the Napoleon had its drawbacks. It was not well adapted to long-range firing. Its range was a mile, but it had little accuracy at that distance. Its trajectory adjustment was limited, which in turn limited its effectiveness with shrapnel. When trajectory is raised, muzzle pressure increases proportionately, thereby increasing the danger of bursting the barrel.

Napoleons had been known to burst, and this worried Robert Parrott. Obviously, the Army needed a gun which would not burst, which had a longer range than the Napoleon, and greater accuracy at all ranges. The latter meant

71

a rifled barrel, higher trajectory and a heavier charge of powder. For a heavier charge, the barrel, especially the butt, must be reinforced.

First, Parrott discarded bronze for steel. After the barrel was bored, it was well rifled. For strength, Parrott shrank a heavy steel sleeve over the butt of the barrel and drilled a hole through both the sleeve and the barrel for igniting the charge.

The Parrott gun, in three-, six- and nine-pounder classes, proved to be the most effective artillery piece of the war. It was reasonably accurate at a mile, especially with conical shells. Its trajectory was raised considerably above the Napoleon, and it placed shrapnel where the gunners wanted it. The gun was superior to anything the Rebels had at the outset of the war, and it proved itself in its introduction to the U.S. Army at Bull Run.

In Civil War battles, the artillery served two basic functions. On the offensive, it was the objective of the artillery to silence the enemy's artillery, thus reducing its fire power against the offense. On the defensive, it was used against the approaching infantry. In both cases a variety of ammunition was employed, depending on the terrain or the range.

In trying to silence the enemy's guns, solid shot might be used to wreck the gun carriages if the distance was not too great for such accuracy. At a longer range, shrapnel might be used to drive the enemy gunners away from their field pieces. The shrapnel shell had a thin metal case, sawed through at several points to weaken it, and filled with bullets, bits of scrap iron and a medium charge of powder. In the base of the shell, the artillery officer inserted a time fuse which resembled a domestic electric fuse. Inside the time fuse there was a coil of cord impregnated with powder and chemicals. Before inserting the fuse, the officer computed the range of his target and clipped the cord to the correct length. With the firing of the cannon, the fuse was ignited. The objective was to have the shell explode just over the heads of the enemy.

On the defensive, shrapnel could be used up to a point, but as the enemy came near, the artillery switched to cannister. The cannister shell was usually made of cardboard and loaded with bullets like a modern shotgun shell, except the whole shell was fired, leaving nothing in the barrel. The use of cannister was the equivalent of heavy machine-gun fire in modern warfare.

Although the artillery was organized into regiments, it was detached to serve with infantry regiments and brigades. The basic unit of the artillery was the battery, consisting of six guns in the North, but more often four in the South. The usual distribution of artillery was one battery to a brigade.

Another artillery weapon, which did not have wide use in the war but was very effective in certain situations, was the howitzer. The Civil War howitzer was a bronze, smoothbore cannon with a short, heavy barrel and a high trajectory. The howitzers of the New Orleans Washington Artillery worked effectively at point-blank range with cannister on the first day of Bull Run. The howitzer also had the ability to lob a concussion shell over a hill to drop on an ammunition dump or a supply base. It was most effective in trench warfare. In this it was more practical than the Civil War mortar, which was so heavy it could not be mounted on a gun carriage and thus was useless except in siege operations.

These weapons—the Springfield, the Colt .44, the John Brown carbine, the Napoleon twelve-pounder, the Parrott and the howitzer—saw action on July 21, 1861.

CHAPTER SEVEN

ON TO RICHMOND!
ON TO WASHINGTON!

FROM the day of Jefferson Davis's inauguration, Southern orators and news-papers had been screaming, "On to Washington!" In the North, after the shelling of Fort Sumter, a much larger chorus chanted, "On to Richmond!" The loudest voice was that of Horace Greeley, editor of the New York *Tribune,* who had only recently said, "Let the wayward daughters go in peace." On both sides, the pressures on the two presidents mounted until it could no longer be politically resisted. The Battle of Bull Run was the result. And it certainly should not have been fought that July, 1861.

Jefferson Davis was in a better position to resist pressure for military action than was Abraham Lincoln. Davis was a military man and Lincoln was not. In the South, the opinions of military men were respected in military matters. In the North, with the possible exception of General Scott, the opinion of a

West Point graduate was given no more credence than that of the general-store owner who commanded the local militia company.

The fact was that in early May, 1861, the Confederacy was in no condition to go "on to Washington" or anywhere else. It had no army, only a collection of unrelated militia regiments around Richmond. It had as yet no supreme commander. In Washington there was a similar hodge-podge of militia with not more than two regiments of regular troops. As supreme commander, Lincoln had a wheel-chair general who believed that the flintlock rifle was still an admirable weapon.

But Lincoln had one argument that could temporarily, at least, silence the "on to Richmond" chorus. The Virginia convention had adopted an ordinance of secession on April 18, and Virginia immediately took on the appearance of a seceded state. Robert E. Lee resigned his commission in the U.S. Army, as did several other Virginia officers. The Virginia delegation in the Congress of the United States went home, and the Virginia militia was alerted. In practice, Virginia had seceded, but Lincoln was able to point out that the Virginia Secession Ordinance provided that it must be ratified by the voters of Virginia at a referendum, and the date of that referendum was May 23. Therefore, wisely perhaps but disastrously for building an army, Lincoln backed General Scott in withholding Union troops from Virginia soil until the results of the referendum were known. The President was 99 percent sure that the ordinance would be ratified, but there was the slim chance of a negative vote, which would not occur if Union troops moved into Virginia.

May 23 came, and the result was as Lincoln had expected. Now there was no excuse for not moving into the Old Dominion. It would provide room for training an army which in six months must be prepared to march on Richmond. But Lincoln knew that the politicians would not let him wait that long. In Virginia, Major General Robert E. Lee, commanding the state militia, but as yet without rank in the Confederate Army, had scattered training camps around

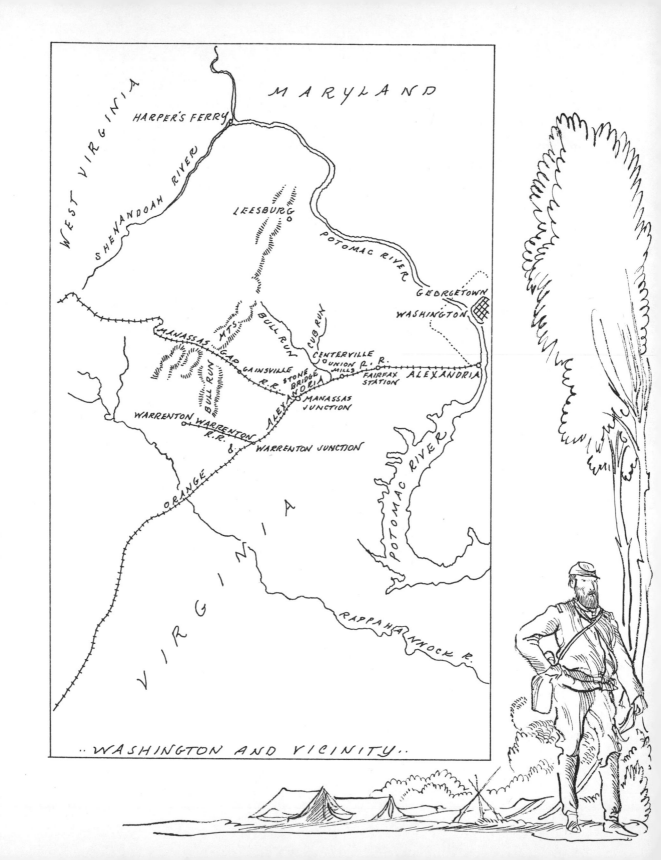

WASHINGTON AND VICINITY

Richmond, Fairfax Court House and Alexandria, but had not yet erected fortifications.

On the morning of May 24, the day after the ratification of the Virginia Ordinance of Secession, the general movement of federal troops began. The march started before daybreak while Washington secessionists were asleep. At 3:00 A.M., U.S. Cavalry troops were posted at the Virginia end of Long bridge on the road to Alexandria. New York regiments crossed the Aqueduct in Georgetown. Other regiments crossed Chain Bridge, west of Georgetown. And Colonel Ellsworth with his exuberant New York Fire Zouaves, accompanied by the First Michigan, took off in a steamboat for Alexandria.

With the army out of Washington, the commanding officers and the people of Washington heaved sighs of relief. Now there was room for everybody. Regiments laid out roomy, sanitary camps, as many unfit militia colonels were replaced by Regular Army men. There was room for maneuvers, and General Scott was too feeble to care whether they were held or not. He was now scheduled for retirement.

But Scott was not replaced as supreme commander until Ulysses S. Grant was given the commission after the Battle of Gettysburg. However, the command of the new Army of the Potomac was placed in the hands of Major Irvin McDowell, with the rank of brigadier general. Some mystery clouds the choice of McDowell. He was born in Franklin, Ohio, in 1818, and graduated from West Point in the class of 1838. He was still only a lieutenant when the army went into Mexico in 1846. There he was brevetted a captain for bravery at the Battle of Buena Vista. By 1861, McDowell had risen to major but had seldom commanded more than a company. Under General Scott's plan for the defense of government buildings in case of an invasion, McDowell was to have commanded a small force of District of Columbia Militia and armed government clerks at the Capitol.

McDowell had received his brigadier's commission while Colonel William

Tecumseh Sherman was in Washington, visiting his brother John, and Colonel Ambrose Burnside was commanding the first Rhode Island. Both officers out-ranked McDowell, were West Point graduates and had had more experience in command. Upon receiving his commission, McDowell moved across the Potomac and set up headquarters in the Lee mansion.

And now came the first casualty of the war, one which shocked Washington and the whole North. Colonel Ellsworth's Fire Zouaves landed at Alexandria without opposition. It was barely daylight, and for once the "Zoozoos" were not whooping it up. The occupation was to be made as quietly as possible. It was soon evident that there were no Confederate troops in the vicinity, and the work of the Zouaves and the First Michigan would be simple guard duty.

For weeks, Washington, especially the War Department, had been irked by the sight of a Confederate flag flying from the cupola of the Marshall House, Alexandria's leading hotel. The flag could be seen with a telescope from the South Portico of the White House.

Upon landing at the City Wharf in Alexandria, Ellsworth took six of his toughest Zouaves and went directly to the Marshall House. Entering the hotel, Ellsworth and his men were greeted by the desk clerk. Ellsworth asked if he were the proprietor and the answer was negative. Then the Colonel took one private and climbed the stairs to the roof where he removed the flag and tucked it under his arm.

When Ellsworth reached the landing on the second floor, James Jackson, the proprietor of the Marshall House, stepped from his bedroom with a double-barreled shotgun. Ellsworth did not see him and called to his men below, "Look, I have the first prize." "And I the second," called out Jackson, firing both barrels point-blank at Ellsworth. Before Ellsworth fell dead, his aide fired, striking Jackson in the center of his forehead. In blind rage and grief, the Zouave pinned the dead proprietor's body to the floor with his bayonet.

When the squad of Zouaves brought Ellsworth's corpse back to the main

The Marshall House—
Alexandria, Virginia

body of troops, there was an uproar of rage. The New Yorkers wanted to burn the whole city, but they were restrained by the colonel of the First Michigan who was now in command of both regiments. The next day, Colonel Ellsworth's body lay in state in the East Room of the White House. Mrs. Lincoln laid flowers on the coffin.

With the Army in the fields of Virginia, real training began for the regiments in Washington, and the green troops began to learn the routine of an army camp. *Reveille* was sounded at 5 A.M. Fifteen minutes later, *Assembly* was blown and the men stumbled out of their tents in various stages of dress and undress. Roll call followed and then sick call. Breakfast call brought the regiment to the cook tents where each man was given a slab of uncooked salt pork and a ration of ground coffee. Now the men returned to their camp fires to cook the meal. Breakfast over, part of the regiment was detailed to gather firewood while the rest drilled. Dinner call came at noon. In the afternoon, more drilling or bayonet practice, with *Retreat* at 5:45 P.M.

Had the recruits of 1861 known what the army would require them to carry and what it would weigh, the gadget salesmen back home would have gone hungry. But every militia camp had swarmed with men selling "you don't know when it might come in handy." Most popular was a knife-fork-spoon combination which clipped together when not in use. (Of course, the Army furnished its own mess kit.) Some salesmen peddled compasses which were said to be indispensable to the soldier who wanted to know where he was going. There were several styles of rubber water filters. Two would have supplied a regiment, but several men in each company had one apiece. They were all thrown away in July between Alexandria and Bull Run.

Many employers presented the men who were leaving for the Army with fine revolvers, ignorant of the regulation that only commissioned officers and cavalry could carry them. The recruit, Yank or Reb, who did not buy or get a gift of a bowie knife to hack his way through to Richmond or Washington was a freak. The acme of gadgetry was the armored vest. In spite of its weight, it sold like hotcakes at $12.00. It became the current cliché to ask a vest owner whether he wore it on his chest or his back. Ridicule, Virginia heat and the weight of the vests soon caused them to be secretly discarded.

In some ways an army was beginning to shape up, but all was not smooth as yet. There was a mutiny in the Garibaldi Guards of New York, causing the unit to be sent home in disgrace. Security measures were virtually nonexistent. Sentries slept at their posts; the offense was punishable by death, but the penalty was not enforced by militia colonels who were seeking re-election. A general could walk through camp after camp at night without receiving a single challenge.

Back at Arlington House, Lee's mansion, somber Irvin McDowell pondered over his problems and tried to plan a campaign. The food supply was slow in coming in from the Quartermaster General, and there were reliable reports that the troops were pillaging the Virginia countryside. McDowell's orders were that any food, forage or firewood taken from a Virginia citizen should be reported and the owner given a voucher payable by the War Department. But a hungry Vermonter who saw a chicken crossing the road wasn't interested in War Department vouchers, and a stray hog was fair game for target practice.

Then there was the problem of horses. The artillery, the commissary and the cavalry needed different kinds of horses. The army had traditionally relied on mules for its wagon trains, and the supply had come mainly from Missouri and Arkansas. The latter had now seceded and Missouri, a border state, was selling most of her mules to the Confederacy. McDowell issued an order limiting six wagons to a regiment. The velvet stools of the New York Seventh would have to be left behind.

Armament was in desperately short supply. In May, Lincoln sent out a call for 200,000 additional volunteers. These were to be Regular Army enlistments for three years. And the states would not arm them. The Springfield Armory was falling behind in the supply of .58 caliber rifles and the Enfield rifles ordered from England had not arrived.

But McDowell's greatest problems were the army under his command and Congress. He knew that his army was far from ready to fight a major battle. He knew the qualities of the Southern West Pointers who would become generals, and the caliber of Southern soldiers. He knew that the editorial predictions of Northern newspapers and congressmen that Richmond could be taken in two weeks were pure wishful thinking or ignorance.

McDowell faced the fact that most of the troops under his command were the three-month enlistments which had answered Lincoln's call in April. Most of these enlistments would expire in July, some before. The new recruits that Lincoln had requisitioned in May would not be ready to replace the discharged militia regiments. McDowell also faced the fact that the President had called a special session of Congress to convene on July 4. The first meeting of the Military Affairs committees of both Houses would bombard the President, Secretary of War Cameron and McDowell with "Why aren't we in Richmond yet?" Yes, a battle would have to be fought in July.

McDowell knew that a Confederate army was encamped somewhere around Manassas Junction. (Manassas Junction, thirty miles from Washington, was strategically located because the Manassas Gap and Orange and Alexandria railways were joined there). Scouts had reported that the tracks of the Orange & Alexandria Railroad had been torn up north of a creek which the natives called Bull Run. Scouts had also encountered Confederate troops as near as Falls Church, but in small detachments. McDowell believed that his only course was to confront the Rebel army somewhere around Manassas Junction, for the reason that the finest road in that section of Virginia, the Warrenton Turnpike, led there. But there was one remaining problem, and a big one: the United States Army did not own an accurate map of Virginia.

CHAPTER EIGHT

THE SKIRMISHES:
BIG BETHEL, RICH MOUNTAIN

ALTHOUGH General Winfield Scott's body was wracked with pain and his training tactics were those of 1812, his grand strategy was as sound as it had been at Mexico City. With an assembled but untrained army, he pinpointed the vulnerability of Virginia to invasion. There were four points: the part of Virginia which is now West Virginia, where the people were unfriendly to the Confederate cause; the Shenandoah Valley which could be invaded from Pennsylvania; Manassas Junction, easily reached via the Warrenton Turnpike; and Fortress Monroe on the tip of Virginia Peninsula which commanded traffic on the York and James Rivers. If the politicians and the press had permitted Scott to wait until he could place trained armies at these four points, Virginia could have been crushed in a giant nutcracker.

Scott had part of his plan in motion as early as May 1. Regiments from western New York and Pennsylvania were already massed at Chambersburg, Pennsylvania. This force would retake Harper's Ferry and focus on the Shenandoah Valley. Next on Scott's agenda was Fort Monroe. With this move he planned to kill or maim two birds with one stone. He had evidence that the Fort could be taken without a battle because there were no Confederate troops in the vicinity.

His second objective was to get Brigadier General Butler as far as possible from Washington and the War Department. This was due to Butler's crude actions, which needlessly upset the people where he was stationed. One example is what happened after the Baltimore riot. When the temper of the Marylanders had cooled after the Baltimore riot, Scott had sent Butler to Baltimore with a brigade to search quietly for allegedly concealed arms intended for shipment to the Confederacy; also he was to be ready to repel an invasion of Maryland from Harper's Ferry if it should come.

Almost immediately, Butler had stirred up a hornet's nest by arresting prominent citizens, bursting into people's homes without search warrants, and parading as much military pomp as his command could provide. Butler was unwittingly schooling himself for his occupation of New Orleans in 1862 where he stepped up enormously his usual crass behavior.

After this Baltimore maneuver, Scott relieved Butler of his command. But Old Cockeye, who demanded military protocol from his subordinates, exercised little of it himself. He immediately stormed the office of Secretary of War Cameron and went from there to the White House. Cameron and Lincoln, realizing that Butler was the Democratic leader of Massachusetts, commissioned him a major general in the Regular Army and handed him back to Scott for disposal.

So Scott had the problem of a command for Butler, who now held the highest rank, under his own, in the Army. Fort Monroe was the place for him, the General decided. Since it could be taken without opposition, Scott could give Butler enough men to hold the fort with ease, and Butler's duties would be mainly administrative, simply waiting for the day when Scott would send a

General Benjamin F. Butler

force to invade the Peninsula, with the fort as its base. Even if Butler treated the Virginia populace as he had the Marylanders, he could not make them any angrier than they were already.

On the day of Virginia's secession, a flotilla of side-wheel or passenger ships and a freighter transported General Butler and about 8,000 men to Fort Monroe, where, as predicted, they landed without a Rebel in sight. Butler found the fort in bad shape but soon had everything in apple-pie order. The water supply inside the fort had a capacity for only 400 men so he had an artesian well drilled outside the fort which would supply his command. Next he began to reconnoiter the countryside. Traveling up the James River aboard a small ship provided by the Navy, he discovered a 60-foot elevation which, if armed, could shut off any Confederate shipping. He went ashore and found it occupied by a farm house and a wheat field. Today the area is the site of the great naval base, Newport News.

After becoming reasonably acquainted with the terrain around Monroe, Butler began to feel the itch for military glory, something worth reporting in the Boston newspapers. Here he had a stout command with no enemy nearer than Norfolk, and he was right in judging that he had enough men to overcome any opposition.

Richmond was immediately aware of Butler's presence. The citizens did not expect a move up the Peninsula at this time, but if heavy artillery were installed at Newport News, Federal battleships could steam up the James River to almost within cannon range of Richmond. Something had to be done about it right away.

General Lee selected Colonel John Bankhed ("Prince John") Magruder as the man for the job. Magruder had graduated from West Point in 1830. During the Mexican War, his brilliant command of an artillery battery had won him steady promotion so that he came out of the war a lieutenant colonel, a most uncommon speed of advancement. Following the war, Magruder was stationed at Fort Adams, Newport, Rhode Island, where he was known for his flashy dress parades and the elegant dinners which followed them. Then he was given command of the Army's artillery school at Leavenworth, Kansas. Magruder was considered the most expert artillery officer in the U.S. Army.

On May 21, Magruder proceeded to Yorktown with a force of 8,000 where he was soon joined by one of the South's most highly trained regiments, the First North Carolina under Colonel D. H. Hill. Magruder had so much confidence in Hill and his Tarheels that he sent them thirteen miles below Yorktown to Big Bethel Church on the Bark River. With them went a battery of four guns.

Soon Butler's scouts spotted the First North Carolina and reported back to the General. They reported erroneously that Hill had 2,000 men behind a fortification; actually, he had somewhat over 1,000, counting his artillery, behind scanty entrenchments. Butler immediately wrote to Scott asking for artillery and cavalry which he did not have. Scott let the letter go unanswered. He had purposely withheld artillery and cavalry, because he did not intend for Butler to take the offensive, but only to hold the fort.

Butler's plan of battle was intricate for so small an engagement. His orders could only have been followed by experienced commanders and seasoned troops. Often they were inexplicit: "March to be hurried but not rapid." The orders stipulated that two regiments should proceed to Little Bethel, site of a Negro church. There Butler expected at least token opposition. One regiment was to march from Newport News and the other from Camp Hamilton, just outside the fort. The orders stated that the regiments were to march in two columns, but did not say whether they were to be parallel columns or one behind the other. They were to march by night or in the dusk of early morning. Butler, having given these orders, chose to remain at the fort, where they could not be countermanded if anything went wrong.

The march went as scheduled until the lead regiment reached Little Bethel.

There in the semidarkness, Colonel Duryea saw another regiment marching parallel to his. Believing it to be Confederate, he ordered his men to fire. The fire was returned, and more men were killed than died in the coming skirmish. The other regiment was from Newport News. Now, with the firing, a surprise attack on Big Bethel was out of the question.

Butler's orders were for the first regiment reaching the Confederate line to fire a volley and take the earthwork by the bayonet. But when Butler's men got within range of the well-served Confederate artillery, they retreated into the woods, firing from behind trees. Several officers were killed and now it was a question of who was in command. No one was. Companies became separated from their commands and confusion reigned. Finally, the remaining officers, agreeing that their commands were disorganized beyond repair, returned to Fort Monroe.

Butler, who refused to accept any blame for the debacle, received the reports of his officers with disgust. They reported that they could not charge with the bayonet, because the Rebel rampart was thirty feet high, and without artillery, they could not stand up to the "thirteen guns" of the enemy. As we know, Hill had four guns, and two days later, Butler rode his horse over the now deserted "thirty-foot rampart." In all, there were seventy-six Union casualties, mainly caused by Union rifles.

There was great jubilation in Richmond as Magruder's report of Big Bethel was received. The skirmish was blown up by the press as the first major battle of the war, in which Magruder and Hill had overcome tremendous odds. The two colonels were now on a par with Lee and Beauregard in public esteem. In the North, newspapers vilified Butler for the loss, condemning him for sending raw troops against such withering rifle fire. Once more Butler was relieved of his command and recalled to Washington.

With a firm base established at Fort Monroe, available for a possible invasion of the Virginia Peninsula, General Scott turned his attention to western Virginia. This was the Confederacy's most vulnerable frontier at the moment. Union sympathy among the mountaineers had brought Confederate enlistments to a standstill. This characteristic of Southern mountain folk was to plague the Confederacy throughout the war. From the foot of the Appalachians in Georgia, through Tennessee, North Carolina and western Virginia, small farmers, who held no slaves and who could barely support their families, had no interest in states' rights or secession. They wanted to be left alone to keep things as they had been. Therefore, troops for the defense of these regions had to be transferred from centers where they were badly needed.

Scott's first objective was to protect the branch of the Baltimore & Ohio Railroad which ran from Washington to Parkersburg. His second was to clear all Confederate forces from western Virginia, if possible. Finally, though this was only a hope at the time, Scott wanted to drive south and take Staunton, which would give him another route to Richmond.

On May 24, Scott placed George B. McClellan in command of the western Virginia department. He was later to command the Army of the Potomac until Lincoln removed him, saying McClellan "had the slows." At the time McClellan received his orders from Scott, he was in command of the Department of Ohio which included Ohio, Indiana, Illinois and western Pennsylvania. This post was then important because of widespread subversive activity in the southern counties of Indiana, Illinois and Ohio.

There was no better trained officer in the U.S. Army than George Brinton McClellan. He was born in Philadelphia, where his father was a doctor, and when he graduated from the U.S. Military Academy in 1846, he left immediately for Mexico as second lieutenant in the Engineers. Coming out of Mexico as a first lieutenant, McClellan was assigned to teach practical engineering at West Point. There, Jefferson Davis, then Secretary of War, selected him to go with a party of army engineers to survey a route for a transcontinental railroad. [This railroad was not completed until 1869.] In 1855, McClellan was sent to

Europe with a mission of officers to obtain information on troop training methods, supply, organization and transportation. While there, he was also assigned as observer for the U.S. Army during the Crimean War. In the Crimea, he saw the most modern armament in operation.

Returning from Europe a captain, McClellan resigned his commission to become president of the Eastern Division of the Ohio & Mississippi Railroad. At the time Lincoln called for volunteers, he was living in Cincinnati.

On June 21, General McClellan entered Parkersburg with five Ohio and two Indiana regiments, three companies of regular artillery and a few companies of state militia cavalry. According to a letter from McClellan to his wife, they were all superbly equipped. By the morning of June 23 McClellan's army was in Grafton, and not a Confederate soldier had been sighted. There he waited four days for his wagon train to catch up. And now McClellan used something which he had learned in Europe and which General Scott would have frowned upon had he heard about it. He had built a military telegraph line from Parkersburg to Grafton. During the wait at Grafton, McClellan picked up another brigade of infantry, and he put the troops he already had through strenuous maneuvers European style. As a result, he probably had the best-trained troops in either army.

Richmond received the news of McClellan's presence the day he marched into Grafton. Colonel George Porterfield, a veteran of the Mexican War, was assigned to recruit an army which would at least try to prevent McClellan from taking the junction of the Staunton–Parkersburg Turnpike at Beverly.

The army which Colonel Porterfield assembled would have horrified most regular army officers. The weapons were a miscellany of ancient flintlock hunting rifles and shotguns; there was only one piece of artillery; and the baggage train was a collection of old farm wagons. The troops were thoroughly raw; there was no time to teach them the manual of arms; and orders had to be given in laymen's language ("Shoot" instead of "Fire"). To handle this motley crew of riflemen would require a skilled and understanding officer.

The man chosen for what seemed a hopeless task was Colonel Garnett, Lee's Adjutant General. Lee was loath to spare him, but there was no other officer of Garnett's ability available at the moment. He had been instructor in tactics at West Point and had won his major's leaves at the Battle of Buena Vista in the Mexican War.

Garnett passed into the Kanawha Valley via the Staunton–Parkersburg Turnpike and took a position on Rich Mountain overlooking Cheat Valley. This position, Garnett thought, would enable him to command Buckhannon Pass, over which he had just marched, and which he considered the "gate to northwestern Virginia." Garnett admitted that his 4,000 untrained troops could not possibly defeat McClellan in open battle, but he thought that by a series of swoops down the mountain on sections of McClellan's army, he might discourage the Yankee general from pushing farther.

Most of Garnett's officers were as untrained as the men they commanded, but there was one exception, Lieutenant Colonel John Pegram. Only twenty-nine years old, Pegram had served as first lieutenant of the U.S. Second Dragoons. He was a thoroughly professional soldier, and as Garnett's second in command, he laid out Camp Garnett at the western entrance to Buckhannon Pass strictly according to army regulations, although it was occupied by raw unprofessional soldiers.

Neither Pegram nor Garnett had very much knowledge of the terrain on which they were encamped, and there was no time to explore the area. Garnett's first move was to set his men to felling trees across all secondary roads which he would not need, believing that this would prevent him from being flanked.

Below the peak of Buckhannon Pass was Laurel Hill, and here Garnett set up a series of low log forts. With youthful confidence in his untrained recruits,

Garnett reported to Richmond on the forts and his men: "They will be able to hold five times their number in check for a sufficient time to admit of being re-inforced, if they will stand to their work."

The forts were quiet until July 8, when Federal skirmishers appeared, but not in force. Skirmishing continued for the next two days, causing Garnett to underestimate the size of McClellan's force. Then on July 11, a captured Union sergeant admitted under questioning that McClellan planned to try a flanking movement and gave some indication of Federal strength. It was Garnett's opin-ion that, if the sergeant was telling the truth, the attack would come on his right. However, to present some opposition if he were wrong, he sent five under-manned companies and a light cannon to his left rear.

Left rear was where the attack came. One by one the artillerymen serving the lone cannon were picked off. Captain de Lagnel, commanding this sector, served the gun himself, with the aid of a young infantryman who had never seen a cannon loaded. Then de Lagnel was hit and severely wounded. He could no longer command.

Now, without even the meager support of one gun, the untrained infantry broke and took shelter in the woods. The Union infantry swarmed over the Buckhannon Pass road, and Garnett's only route of retreat was cut off. There was only one small chance of saving this ill-fated Confederate army. Half of Garnett's command was defending Camp Garnett, the other half had been driven down the mountain on the other side of the Pass. One more attempt could be made to drive the Federals off Buckhannon Pass. But the men, already exhausted in battle, were useless for further fighting by the time they had climbed back up the mountain through a thick cover of laurel. Instead, they threw themselves on the ground in the woods to rest and sleep.

By the next morning, Garnett's little army was hopelessly scattered. Moving in the night, detachments had lost contact, and now they were strewn over both sides of Rich Mountain, with their wagon train in the hands of McClellan's men. Pegram was cut off from his food supply and his ammunition was all but exhausted. He sent a messenger to McClellan's headquarters and surrendered 533 men and officers on July 13.

Garnett managed to get the remaining troops to Kaler's Ford on the Cheat River, only to find the Federals approaching. To slow their crossing of the ford, he posted ten sharpshooters in a pile of driftwood on the river bank. At the first shot from a sharpshooter, the Federal advance guard opened fire. Garnett was standing just above the driftwood, directing his men and since he was the only enemy visible, he became the target. As he turned on his horse to see if the remainder of his troops were moving up, a bullet struck him in the back. He died shortly afterward, depriving the South of its most promising young general.

Most of Garnett's remaining command escaped, but the loss of 700 men killed, taken prisoner, or wounded was a staggering blow. The Battle of Rich Mountain ended the Confederacy's attempt to hold western Virginia and the section soon became the State of West Virginia.

But the people of both sides back home were still yelling "On to Richmond," "On to Washington."

CHAPTER NINE

"BORY'S HERE"

THE shouts went up and down the streets of Richmond on May 31, 1861: "Old Bory's here!" "Beauregard is at the depot." "There's goin' t'be a big parade." At the railroad station, General Pierre Gustave Toutant Beauregard was stepping down from the wooden passenger coach, accompanied by a fellow Louisianian, Judah P. Benjamin, who had come along to assume the duties of Secretary of War in the Davis Cabinet. The wood-burning locomotive was spewing sparks and steam over the almost hysterical crowd of Richmond ladies, volunteer firemen, tobacco merchants, soldiers and members of the Confederate Congress. It was a gala day.

The "hero of Fort Sumter" was forty-three years old. Born in St. Bernard Parish [County], just down the river from New Orleans, he had graduated from West Point, *cum laude,* in the class of 1838 and made the Army his career. During the Mexican War he held the rank of captain in the U.S. Engineer Corps and was later brevetted major for bravery. Since his "victory" at Fort

94

Sumter, Beauregard had been stationed at Pensacola, Florida. But with the invasion of Virginia by the Federals, the general had been summoned by President Davis to command the Confederate army there.

At this point the relationship between Beauregard and Robert E. Lee becomes rather confusing. When Lee resigned from the U.S. Army, Governor Letcher of Virginia commissioned him major general in command of all Virginia troops and all military operations in the state. Before the Battle of Bull Run, no officer in the Confederate Army held a rank above brigadier general. The Virginia troops which Lee was to command had been sworn into the Confederate Army which was under the command of Beauregard. At the same time, Lee outranked Beauregard. It took several months and a feud between Beauregard and President Davis to place Lee in supreme command of the Army of Northern Virginia. This partly explains why Robert E. Lee, the South's greatest military genius, was not at the Battle of Bull Run.

As Beauregard detrained, the crowd shouted for a speech. The general, who could use elegant language when he wanted to, pretended modesty. He shook his head, and nodded in the direction of Judah Benjamin. Benjamin, a brilliant lawyer who had represented Louisiana in the U.S. Senate, gave a rousing oration in which he predicted that Beauregard would repeat his glorious victory at Fort Sumter, and bring peace within a matter of weeks.

Four sleek horses drew a luxurious carriage up to the station platform and a band took its place up front. Again Beauregard shook his head. He wanted a less conspicuous vehicle, and he wanted to ride alone. The officials assented, but a cheering crowd and the band followed the new hero up the hill to the Spotswood Hotel where Beauregard had reserved a suite and where President Davis was staying temporarily.

Beauregard, little known outside the Army prior to his bloodless bombardment of Fort Sumter in April, had become a legend in six weeks. He had been thanked by the Confederate Congress, newspaper editorials ranked him with the great military heroes of the world, and there were those who believed that he was the reincarnation of Napoleon. There was one story that he had notified President Lincoln to have all civilians out of Washington by a certain date because he would occupy the city on that day.

The morning after Beauregard's arrival in Richmond, there was a conference of four complex and widely divergent personalities: President Davis, Lee, Beauregard and Benjamin. Davis was unhappy. He had wanted to lead the Army in person as Commander-in-Chief. As mentioned earlier, he was a West Point graduate and had been a lieutenant in the U.S. Army, a colonel in the Mexican War and Secretary of War under President Pierce. He believed himself qualified above all the others for supreme command. The Confederate Congress said, "No."

Lee, the Virginia aristocrat, a professional soldier who had resigned from the U.S. Army with the rank of colonel, was definitely the best qualified for supreme command. He had outranked Beauregard in the Old Army and outranked him now. But Lee was too humble and too much a gentleman to "throw his weight around." He would take any post assigned him.

Judah P. Benjamin always wore a faint smile. One of the nation's greatest lawyers, he became Queen's Counsel to Queen Victoria after the war ended and he had escaped via the West Indies. As a Jew, he met the racial discrimination of the nineteenth century with his well-known smile and a shrug of his broad shoulders. He was not happy over his appointment as Secretary of War for the Confederacy; when he later became Confederate Secretary of State he conducted a brilliant but fruitless campaign to obtain diplomatic recognition of the Confederacy by the European powers.

Beauregard was already beginning to believe that he was a military genius and that those who said he was the reincarnation of Napoleon might possibly be right. Small in stature like Napoleon, he had high cheekbones, sallow skin and the sad eyes of a bloodhound. He wore a small mustache and goatee. Although reserved in appearance and speech, he became grandiose and somewhat pompous in his correspondence.

What was said at this momentous conference was never recorded, nor was the authority of Lee and Beauregard defined, but Davis gave Beauregard the direct responsibility for defending Virginia, from the Potomac River south to Richmond. However, his jurisdiction did not extend to the Shenandoah Valley. This left Lee as little more than military adviser to President Davis (who did not want any advice at the moment) but with responsibility for the Virginia Peninsula.

Another positive result of the conference was that Beauregard should establish headquarters at Manassas Junction where several thousand Confederate troops were already encamped. Manassas Junction, although only a village, was of great strategic importance, either for attack or defense. It lay just off the Warrenton Turnpike which led south from Alexandria. While the "pike" was no throughway, it was a better-than-average road by the standards of the day. It would be the main thoroughfare for any army moving toward or from Washington. The village sat on rather high ground above the neighboring countryside, making it ideal for entrenchment. As a railroad junction, it was a perfect location for quickly assembling men and supplies, and this was to prove one of the decisive factors in the battle of July 21.

Finally, there was Bull Run. Bull Run was not any great shakes as a waterway, but it provided a strong defensive position. Along most of its course it was not more than thirty feet wide and its flow was sluggish. In July, the water would hardly be more than a foot deep. Its defensive strength lay in its almost perpendicular banks of stratified rock, rising at least ten feet except at natural or man-made fords. In addition to the fords there was Stone Bridge, a part of the Warrenton Turnpike. The bridge was for one-way traffic only, and therefore could be defended against a brigade by a battalion of infantry and a couple of cannon firing cannister.

Bull Run

The final advantage of Manassas Junction consisted of the Bull Run Mountains. Part of the Blue Ridge chain, those not so high but very steep mountains provided a formidable defense against an attack from the Shenandoah Valley, although General Beauregard never really seems to have understood this. There is no passage over the Bull Run Mountains except through a few passes called "gaps" (Snickers Gap, Manassas Gap, and others). Like Stone Bridge, these gaps could be defended by a handful of men.

But one factor, which had nothing to do with the terrain of Manassas Junction, but which was of extreme importance, was the rickety little Manassas Gap Railroad. As long as the Confederate Army controlled the Shenandoah Valley, troops could be shuttled back and forth as needed, and at Bull Run they were sorely needed. Even if the valley fell into the hands of the Federals, Beauregard could tear up the tracks, burn the bridges and easily defend the Gap.

Beauregard left Richmond for Manassas Junction the morning after the conference with Lee, Davis and Benjamin. His route reveals the movement of troops and supplies from the Confederate capital to the Manassas rallying point. Beauregard and his staff boarded the "cars" on the Richmond, Fredericksburg & Potomac Railroad to Hanover Junction, where they transferred to the Virginia Central which took them to Orange and thence to Manassas Junction via the Orange & Alexandria Railroad.

If this sounds like a complicated way to travel perhaps seventy miles, it should be remembered that in 1861 there were almost no great railroad systems. A group of investors raised enough money to build a railroad from A to B. They had no money to go farther. But at B, another group of venturesome capitalists raised enough money to build a railroad from B to C. The two lines might have connecting tracks, but at each terminal the traveler, whether a planter or a brigadier general, had to detrain and buy another ticket. This was normal in both the North and the South, and few railroads owned trackage of over 200 miles.

Arriving at Manassas, General Beauregard requisitioned a dwelling house and called for a review of all the troops in the vicinity. To the "Great Creole" the review foretold both good and ill. The troops at Manassas were the regiments and companies which had enlisted first. They were reasonably well disciplined and handled themselves well in the field. The command was also quite good by West Point standards.

The senior officer was Colonel Milledge Bonham of South Carolina, who had fought in the Seminole and Mexican wars and had represented his state in Congress until its secession. He had brought with him two crack, well-armed South Carolina regiments totaling 1500 men. Colonel J. F. Preston was organizing into a regiment the Virginia recruits who were pouring into Manassas. At Culpepper Court House, performing the same function, was Colonel Philip St. George Cocke, a West Pointer, who had served two years in the army before becoming a wealthy planter. Certainly, Beauregard could not complain of his officers up to this point, while in McDowell's army the Republican town committee chairmen wore the shoulder straps in too many companies and regiments.

But as the flashily uniformed regiments marched smartly past Beauregard in review, he could count only 6,000 men in his command. At the time, he estimated, quite correctly, that McDowell had 30,000. Beauregard immediately returned to his headquarters and dashed off a letter to President Davis: "I must be reinforced at once as I have not more than 6,000 effective men, or I must be prepared to retire on the approach of the enemy in the direction of Richmond with the intention of arresting him whenever and wherever the opportunity shall address itself, or I must march to meet him at one of the fords of Bull Run, to sell our lives as dearly as practicable."

Beauregard's next move was an attempt to inspire and inflame the civilians of the countryside. On June 5, the Napoleon-sized general issued this resounding proclamation: "A restless and unprincipled tyrant has invaded your soil. Abraham Lincoln, regardless of all moral, legal and constitutional restraints, has thrown his abolition hosts among you, who are murdering and imprisoning your citizens, confiscating and destroying your property and committing other acts of violence and outrage too shocking and revolting to humanity to be enumerated, and they proclaim by their acts if not their banners that their war cry is 'Beauty and booty.' All that is dear to man, your honor, and that of your wives and daughters, your fortunes and your lives, are involved in this momentous contest. . . ." He concluded with the exhortation: "I conjure you to be true and loyal to your country and her legal constitutional authorities, and especially to be vigilant of the movements and acts of the enemy, so as to enable you to give the earliest authentic information to these headquarters or to the officers under my command. I desire to assure you that the utmost protection in my power will be extended to you all."

The late Douglas Southall Freeman, that supreme historian of the War Between the States, in the first volume of *Lee's Lieutenants,* places great stress on the last sentence of Beauregard's proclamation, especially on *"in my power."* He questions Beauregard's power to do what he promised. This question was based on Virginia's great vulnerability, more than that of any other Confederate state, to invasion on more than one front. Virginia was already invaded from the north at Arlington Heights and Alexandria. There was the Federal toehold at Fort Monroe. Harper's Ferry was a weak spot for invasion, and finally the Confederate defeat at Rich Mountain had opened up western Virginia to invasion.

Thus, Beauregard was promising the people of the Old Dominion that he could, if necessary, fight a war on four fronts with state militia regiments which had never "seen the elephant," a phrase used in 1861 for being under fire for the first time. There is no record that President Davis or General Lee shared in Beauregard's confidence.

CHAPTER TEN

BEAUREGARD DRAFTS A PLAN

GENERAL Beauregard was becoming more confident every day, and with some reason. His force at Manassas Junction had now swelled to 19,000, with more regiments arriving by the hour. Protecting him from an attack from the Shenandoah Valley was General Joseph E. Johnston with 20,000 men at Harper's Ferry. And there was no sign as yet that McDowell was preparing to advance.

Now for a quick look at Joe Johnston. He was fifty-four years old in July 1861. He had traveled the usual route through West Point (1829), the Indian and Mexican Wars, and had resigned from the U.S. Army with the rank of quartermaster general. He was short, peppery, and already jealous of Beauregard. He considered that, aside from Scott, he was the ranking officer of the U.S. Army at the time of his resignation, and he was annoyed that Davis had sent him off to a temporarily quiet sector with an inferior army.

Beauregard now began bombarding Davis and Lee with plans for a battle.

All except the last were turned down by Davis and Lee as being too complicated for untrained militia colonels or requiring more transportation than was available. All of the plans had one move in common: to join Johnston's command with Beauregard's. But in this combination of two armies, Beauregard had one misgiving. Because Johnston outranked Beauregard, by virtue of the date of his commission in the Old Army, Johnston might insist on taking command and would get the credit for the victory.

Before drafting his alternative plans, Beauregard personally reconnoitered the entire area around Manassas Junction and Bull Run. This was essential, because he had only one map of the vicinity which showed only roads, towns and rivers —not elevations. He found that it was a mile and a half from Manassas Junction to the nearest point on Bull Run. The country between Bull Run, Manassas, and the Warrenton Turnpike was open and rolling. There was a road running west from Manassas to the Turnpike with a stout stone house at the intersection. To the south and west, the country was wooded for the most part.

Beauregard found that Bull Run flowed generally eastward until it joined the Occoquan River, a tributary of the Potomac. The nearest settlement was Centreville, a hamlet on a hill two miles north of Stone Bridge crossing Bull Run. Riding along the Run, Beauregard noted the perpendicular rock banks which were obviously impassable for an army. But he also jotted down on his map that there were seven fords where the water was shallow enough for infantry and artillery. Farthest to the west was Sudley Springs Ford with a narrow road leading to the Turnpike and joining it at the stone house which Beauregard had already seen. Just east of Stone Bridge was Lewis Ford. It could easily be defended, Beauregard decided. Next east, but not connected with a road, was Ball's Ford, then Mitchell's Ford, with a narrow road to Centreville, and Blackburn's Ford, again to the east with a good road to Centreville. Finally, just to the east of the torn-up tracks of the Orange & Alexandria Railroad, lay Union Mills Ford, also with a good road to Centreville.

Beauregard estimated that his battle line would stretch from Stone Bridge to Union Mills Ford, a distance of about five miles This he believed he could defend if Johnston joined him. He also believed that McDowell's army would batter itself to pieces against his defenses, making it possible for him to drive it back to Washington.

Beauregard had done his homework on the fields around Manassas, but he was totally ignorant of the counties of northern Virginia. And he did not know the topography of the Shenandoah Valley, for he had never been there. One of the early plans called for Johnston to join him, and after McDowell had been soundly defeated, to dash back with both Confederate armies to the Valley to check any Federal advance there. He was unaware that the grade was so steep on the Manassas Gap Railroad that the locomotives could pull only a few cars at a time, and that the rickety little railroad did not dash anywhere.

Beauregard knew that facing Johnston at Harper's Ferry was General Patterson with supposedly 30,000 men. He feared that if Johnston came to his aid, Patterson would come charging up the Valley, cross the mountains, get to his rear and block a withdrawal toward Richmond, should one be necessary. Had Beauregard seen the sixty-nine-year-old Patterson in the last ten years, he would have realized that Patterson wouldn't be charging anywhere if he could help it. Secondly, if Beauregard had been familiar with the topography of the Shenandoah Valley and the mountains separating it from his command, as a former army engineer he would have realized that it would take three weeks for an army of 30,000 to move up the Valley and over the mountains.

When Beauregard returned from his reconnaissance, he studied his almost useless map and made a prediction of McDowell's strategy. And if one of McDowell's generals had not made an error of judgment on July 18, Beauregard might have been right. Beauregard took it for granted that McDowell would come directly down the Warrenton Turnpike to Centreville. Since there were three reasonably good roads from there to Mitchell's, Blackburn's, McLean's and

Union Mills fords, McDowell could most easily move his divisions to that part of the line which was Beauregard's right. He concluded, therefore, that he would have to mass his strength there.

Beauregard was happy to fight on this terrain. From Bull Run, the fields sloped gently upward, permitting his artillery to fire over the heads of the infantry, and guns with reasonably high trajectory could cover the Turnpike for a mile north of Stone Bridge if there should be an attack at that point.

Now Beauregard got word from Richmond that General Johnston had evacuated Harper's Ferry on June 15 and dropped back to Winchester. This was good news, for it placed Johnston in a position where he could face Patterson more safely. If McClellan should succeed in defeating Garnett (the battle of Rich Mountain had not yet been fought), Johnston had enough men to halt him should he invade the valley. But best of all, it put Johnston only twenty miles from the terminal of the Manassas Gap Railroad. The railroad run was thirty-five miles.

But not all the news from Johnston was good. Although his command was 20,000 on paper, Beauregard learned from Richmond that only 11,000 were effective fighting men—the rest were either ill or unarmed. Beauregard was further warned that Johnston's men were recent enlistments and not as well trained as Beauregard's at Manassas.

After having so many of his battle plans rejected by Davis and Lee, the general finally capitulated and submitted a very simple plan of operation. He would not call for Johnston's troops until he knew that McDowell was well on his way to attack at Bull Run. McDowell might move his army onto the Warrenton Turnpike and then stop at Fairfax Court House for further maneuvers. Beauregard studied a map of the roads out of Washington, Arlington and Alexandria and concluded that for an army now estimated at 35,000 the turnpike would prove to be a bottleneck. Therefore, he could well afford to wait until McDowell reached Fairfax Court House before pulling his advance guard back from Centreville and calling for Johnston.

President Davis happily accepted Beauregard's plan and immediately telegraphed his instructions to Johnston, who confirmed them. Extra railroad equipment was transferred from the Virginia Central, the Richmond, Fredericksburg & Potomac and the Orange & Alexandria to the Manassas Gap line, and Johnston had his wagon trains loaded so he could leave immediately when needed. Fortunately the railroad crossed the turnpike just below Bull Run, so the trains could be unloaded there without having to run into Manassas Junction.

Now only one apparent problem remained for Beauregard. How would he know when McDowell would begin his advance? Beauregard had had the answer to that one for some time.

CHAPTER ELEVEN

BORY GETS THE WORD

IN Washington's Lafayette Square, across the street from the White House and St. John's Church, stood a small, attractive, two-story house, the property of a widow, Rose O'Neal Greenhow. It had been well known before the war that she was a Southern sympathizer, but so was at least half of Washington, so no one thought much about it.

Rose Greenhow knew everyone in Washington who was worth knowing. She attended all of the most exclusive parties, including White House receptions. She was a confidante of senators, cabinet members, Supreme Court justices and Army officers. In the summer of 1861, she was in mourning, having lost one of her two daughters. According to the social dictates of the period, women in mourning should not be seen in public, especially at society functions, and Rose bowed to custom. But if Rose Greenhow could not go out into Washington society, there was nothing to prevent Washington society from coming to her.

Rose O'Neal Greenhow

Among her regular visitors were Secretary of State William Seward, Congressman Charles Francis Adams of Massachusetts, Colonel Keyes of the U.S. Army and Senator Henry Wilson of Massachusetts, a member of the Senate Military Affairs Committee. Still very attractive even in middle age, Rose had many young army officers among her callers. All were charmed by her grace, her witty conversation, her choice of wines and her taste in dress.

Assistant Secretary of War Thomas Scott became worried. Captain Thomas Jordan of the U.S. Army had mysteriously disappeared. He had been on duty at the War Department where he had access to secret files. Now there were rumors that he had deserted to the Confederacy. What worried Scott most was that Jordan, as everyone knew, was an intimate friend of Rose Greenhow.

Scott called in "Major Allen." This was the alias of Allan Pinkerton, head of the U.S. Secret Service, then the espionage agency of the federal government. Scott urged Pinkerton to arrest Mrs. Greenhow on suspicion of treason. Pinkerton checked with his superiors and the answer was "No, not just yet." Unless Pinkerton was armed with unimpeachable evidence, the whole affair might backfire. If he charged into Rose's home with a warrant, who else would he find? Secretary Seward? Senator Wilson?

If the disappearance of Captain Jordan was a mystery to Assistant Secretary of War Scott, it was no mystery to Rose Greenhow. She knew that Captain Jordan was now wearing the uniform of a Confederate colonel as Adjutant General to General Beauregard at Bull Run, eighteen miles away.

Now Jordan paid Rose Greenhow another visit, this time in civilian clothes. Jordan kept a skiff hidden in a clump of bushes on the southern bank of the Potomac River. In the morning mist he had no difficulty in crossing to the Maryland side of the river. There he had breakfast as usual with friends who harbored him on his frequent secret trips into Washington. A short distance from his friends' house there was a livery stable where he hired a horse and buggy.

Lightly disguised, Jordan drove into Washington and straight to the little green house on Lafayette Square. President Lincoln could have seen him had he been looking out of his window. Behind drawn shades, Jordan revealed the purpose of his mission to Rose Greenhow. General Beauregard was quite confident that he knew the size and armament of McDowell's army, but the success of his battle plan would depend on knowing almost precisely when McDowell would leave Alexandria and Arlington Heights to march on Bull Run. He must know when to call Johnston for help, and Johnston must remain at Winchester as late as possible. Rose told Jordan that she did not have the information, but she would get it to Beauregard in a few days.

Rose Greenhow had a social protégé, Bettie Duvall. Bettie was young and beautiful, with gracious manners, always impeccably dressed, and an excellent horsewoman as well. She lived across the Potomac in Virginia. On July 10, this lovely young girl rode away from Rose's home in a farm wagon, disguised as a farmer's wife who had driven into the city to deliver vegetables. Apparently she had used this disguise several times before, because when she came to Chain Bridge leading to the Warrenton Turnpike, she was not stopped by the sentries.

Still within the Union lines and in sight of an army encampment, Bettie stopped at a friend's house. There she changed from her farm costume to a smart riding habit and borrowed a fast horse. Not far down the road she was challenged by the provost guard (military police today), but she dug her spurs into the horse and galloped through. A warning shot was fired over her head, but by now she was nearly out of sight. McDowell had no cavalry in the vicinity to pursue her. At Fairfax Court House, she was hailed by Confederate guards, but she eluded them and sped on to her goal, the headquarters of General Bonham.

At Bonham's headquarters, Bettie Duvall was halted and placed under guard until she produced from her bosom a note written by Rose Greenhow in Confederate code. She was immediately taken to Bonham where, without a word, she removed her snood and let her waist-long hair fall loose. Then she took from her hair a small packet of fine silk neatly folded to the size of a dollar bill. She handed this to General Bonham without a word. Bonham carefully unfolded the silk until it was over a yard square. Examining it he saw a printed map of the territory between Alexandria, Arlington Heights and Manassas Junction. A line of blue dots showed the route which McDowell would take to attack at Bull Run. It also indicated the parallel roads over which McDowell would move his army onto the Turnpike. In the upper left hand corner was written in hand, "July 18, as of now." On the lower corner was printed, "Property—U.S. Senate, Committee on Military Affairs." And on the opposite corner, again in hand—"Present Federal force 32,000. McDowell thinks Johnston will stay in Valley—H." "H" was the Confederate code word for Rose O'Neal Greenhow.

CHAPTER TWELVE

BLUNDER AT HARPER'S FERRY

IN his wheelchair, General Winfield Scott could warm with satisfaction that thus far his grand strategy had worked. Fort Monroe had been successfully occupied. The Rebels had been driven from western Virginia. And now two great armies were poised to drive simultaneously against the Confederacy at Manassas Junction and Harper's Ferry. Yes, the giant pincers were ready to begin the big squeeze. Had everyone carried out their orders it would have happened.

General Patterson was at Chambersburg, Pennsylvania with 22,000 troops. Scott correctly estimated the effective command of General Johnston to be 11,000. Again correctly, Scott predicted that, unless prevented, these troops would go to Beauregard's aid. Therefore, Patterson was ordered to pin down Johnston's army in combat or try to march around him and prevent him from crossing the mountains. It was Scott's plan to have McDowell and Patterson move simultaneously.

The weakness of the whole plan was Scott's choice of a general to face Joe

Johnston. Johnston was at the time second only to Lee in military skill. In his fifties, he was still as alert and crafty as a fox. Patterson, sixty-nine, was indecisive and easily influenced. He was no man to put opposite Johnston. The latter was at Harper's Ferry, heavily intrenched.

To get into position for an attack on Johnston, Patterson moved his army down to Williamsport, on the north bank of the Potomac. There he found that Johnston had mounted heavy cannon, brought up from the Norfolk Navy Yard, to prevent his crossing. Patterson decided to wait there until he received the word to advance from Scott. He waited until his pickets reported that they had not seen a man around the big guns. Patterson now pushed the pickets across the Potomac at this point, which was a few miles west of Harper's Ferry. They reported that the guns were spiked and not a Confederate in sight.

Patterson had to make a decision, a difficult process for the old general. Should he attack Harper's Ferry or wait for orders from General Scott? Patterson assumed that Johnston was still there. Cautiously he moved his army toward the Ferry, expecting an attack at any moment. The army moved slowly. There were flankers in the fields on each side of the road. The advance guard proceeded with bayonets fixed. The artillery and the wagon train were protected by cavalry. Finally Patterson's army reached Harper's Ferry. It was as quiet as a Sunday morning, and not a Confederate within the horizon.

Patterson was stunned. He called for his second in command, General Cadwallader, and his adjutant general, Fitz-John Porter. None of the trio could come up with an explanation. Finally Patterson said, "I believe it is designed for a decoy; there may be some deep-laid plot to deceive us." So the army sat down in Harper's Ferry while Joe Johnston was twenty miles away in Winchester.

Johnston had only put to use his intelligence, good judgment and years of army experience. Along with General Scott, he recognized that Harper's Ferry was of little strategic value. He knew that Patterson could, if he chose, cross the

Potomac above the Ferry (which he did) and march to his rear (which he did not). Furthermore, he had no intention of pitting his 11,000 men against Patterson's 22,000. Thus, he moved up the Shenandoah Valley to Winchester where he would be near the Manassas Gap Railroad.

Finally, when his cavalry scouts reported that they could not find a trace of Johnston's army, Patterson advanced to Martinsburg and from there to Bunker Hill, only nine miles from Winchester. Here the army sat down again to wait for word from Scott. On the morning of July 16, Patterson sent out cavalry scouts who reported that Johnston's army was drawn up in line of battle behind stone walls just north of Winchester.

Patterson's orders had been to pin Johnston down by attacking him or attempt to get to his rear and block him from joining Beauregard. Instead, Patterson chose to retreat to Martinsburg. There, men in civilian clothes began coming into camp saying that they were spies sent out by General Scott. Patterson listened credulously as they told him that they had just come from within Johnston's lines; that he had 42,000 men and 50 cannon. The men had truly come from within Johnston's lines; they were on Johnston's payroll.

Patterson called a council of war. He had received word that McDowell would begin his march the next day, and he believed that he should attack Johnston in spite of his reported numbers. Fitz-John Porter argued against moving. Cadwallader remained silent. In the end, Porter won out. The next morning, McDowell began his march to Bull Run, Johnston was preparing to leave for Manassas Junction and Patterson with his army was retiring to Harper's Ferry.

CHAPTER THIRTEEN

THE LONG SHORT MARCH

12 noon, July 16, 1861. General Tyler's division of the Army of the Potomac began the march to Manassas. The battle flags were bright, the Fire Zouaves were brighter and a band preceded every regiment down the Warrenton Turnpike. Following Tyler came four other divisions: Hinter's, Heintzelman's, Miles's and Runyon's. The army numbered 28,000, with 49 cannon. The weather was blistering, and gradually the roadside was littered with discarded blankets, bowie knives, rubber water filters, "bullet-proof" vests and the revolvers presented by patriotic former employers.

But the army was in a holiday mood. The bands and the fife and drum corps alternated in keeping the air alive with martial music: "Yankee Doodle," "Rally 'Round the Flag, Boys," "The Fire Zouaves March," "Garry Owen," "Peas on a Trencher," "John Brown's Body," "The Girl I Left Behind Me" and "Columbia, the Gem of the Ocean."

Each division commander had orders from General McDowell which concluded: "Three following things will not be pardonable in any commander: to come upon a battery or breastwork without knowledge of its position; to be surprised; to fall back." The first two items of this order reflect the only two fears which the Northern troops had developed up to this point. One was Confederate "masked batteries." Why the men thought that any artillery officer, Rebel or Union, would leave his battery unmasked if he could help it is hard to explain. Then there had been continuous rumors about the horrendous Confederate "Black Horse Cavalry," as though men mounted on white, roan or dappled horses were any less formidable than those on black horses.

Now the march slowed down almost to a halt, and the aversion of the militia regiments to strict military discipline began to tell. Blackberries were ripe, and whole companies of men left the ranks to pick them. When the column came to a stream, no one asked the recently elected colonel's permission to wander off and fill his canteen. After all, there was no hurry, they said. "We'll be in Richmond in a few days and then go home in time to get the hay in." At Germantown, about five miles out of Arlington Heights, a baggage wagon broke down and the driver had to cut the horses' harnesses. The horses galloped down the Turnpike in the direction of Centreville with a company of infantry chasing them in a spirit of good clean fun.

It was also at Germantown that the column came upon a detachment of Rebels with two Napoleon six-pounders, but they vanished upon sight of the advancing troops. General McDowell was both surprised and irked that the press corps had arrived there ahead of his army and had had rewarding interviews with the enemy—rewarding to themselves, not to McDowell.

After having very nearly confronted a masked battery, the weary army encamped. Almost no one in the column had ever marched five miles before. There had been several cases of sunstroke, but no regiment had thought it necessary to bring along a hospital tent. After all, no one was likely to get hurt.

As soon as the Johnny Rebs saw this invincible, dedicated army, they would flee to Richmond or lay down their arms to go home and grow their cotton.

9:00 A.M.*, July 17, 1861.* So the army had marched about seven miles, had gone to bed early and apparently overslept this morning, since the column was not on the march until nine. The farther it crept on, the greater the fear of masked batteries and the Black Horse Cavalry. The march this day was slower than yesterday's, and the roadside continued to be littered with discarded equipment. The regulation army boots, which had been purchased by wheeler-dealer Secretary of War Cameron, were beginning to disintegrate on the feet of the few who had them. And while McDowell's "Boys in Blue" are picking blackberries, let us take a brief look at this Secretary of War.

Simon Cameron, the Pennsylvania Republican boss, became Secretary of War in March 1861 because of a deal, made without Lincoln's knowledge, at the Republican National Convention of 1860. In a day when candidates for the presidential nomination never attended their party's national convention, Abraham Lincoln paid the expenses of Mark Delahay, a Kansas delegate, to be his floor manager. Delahay stopped in Springfield on his way to the Chicago convention. Lincoln's only words were, "No deals under any circumstances."

When Delahay arrived in Chicago, he found that Governor William Seward of New York had a strong lead for the nomination. But there was a faction in the New York delegation, headed by New York *Tribune* editor Horace Greeley, which was opposed to Seward. Delahay also received a tip that Governor Curtin of Pennsylvania had said the Republicans could carry his state by 50,000 votes with anyone but Seward. Then Delahay learned that Simon Cameron, chairman of the Pennsylvania delegation, would throw his state's votes to anyone if he could be the next Secretary of the Treasury. Delahay telegraphed Lincoln who firmly repeated "No deals."

But as Lincoln's votes rose to a point where he was about to pass Seward, Delahay's enthusiasm got the better of him and he made the deal with Cameron.

After Lincoln got the nomination, he was furious at Delahay and refused to give Cameron the Treasury post or any other. However, between the convention and the election, Lincoln relented and agreed to make Cameron Secretary of War. The results were the boots which disintegrated on the way to Bull Run, the impure food which was purchased for the Army at exorbitant prices, and the blankets which fell apart after a rain. Finally, Lincoln had to demand Cameron's resignation.

9:00 A.M., *July 18, 1861.* Again the army did not set foot on the Warrenton Turnpike until nine. After all, the column was within easy marching distance of Centreville where a battle could take place. The bands had to polish their instruments and the generals had to be sure their own uniforms were spic and span. They had read Dufour's *Strategy and Tactics.* Dufour had been one of Napoleon's marshals and his book had been used as a textbook at West Point. It was available of course to militia officers. Dufour prescribed that on the morning of a major battle, officers should wear their dress uniforms and swords, because if the enemy were worthy of being fought, the attacking army should show proper respect by appearing at its best.

CHAPTER FOURTEEN

SEEING THE ELEPHANT

BY noon on July 18, McDowell's army, in apple-pie order, scrubbed and polished, arrived at Centreville. Centreville was only a crossroads hamlet with a general store and a few scattered farm houses. The rest of the immediate countryside consisted of broad fields, an excellent location for an army encampment. McDowell halted and ordered tents pitched.

McDowell seems to have had no detailed plan for attacking Bull Run at this time. He had considered an attack at Stone Bridge, but this was open country and he would have exposed his strength to the enemy. After dinner (noon), he set part of his army to repairing and altering the abandoned Confederate fortifications so the strength would be to the south. These barricades he could use in case he was forced to retire.

Then McDowell ordered Richardson's brigade of Tyler's division to reconnoiter Blackburn's Ford. At this point, things were badly handled all around.

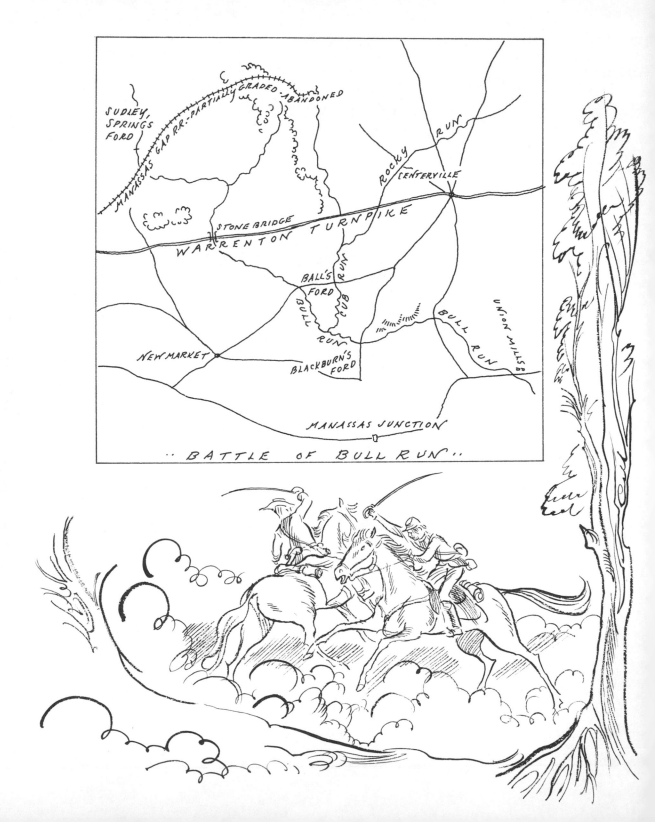

.. BATTLE OF BULL RUN ..

Using an entire brigade to reconnoiter what could have been done just as effectively by a regiment would give the impression that McDowell intended to make his main attack at Blackburn's Ford and allow Beauregard the time to prepare for it. The problem was McDowell's inconclusive orders. He simply ordered Tyler to find out the enemy's strength at the Ford. Such an order could mean two approaches. The first, which was apparently what McDowell had in mind, was a scouting expedition to *observe* the enemy's strength. The second, which was what Tyler thought McDowell meant, was to attack the enemy and see how hard he fought back. Tyler passed McDowell's order on to Richardson who relayed it to the regimental colonels. There was no plan. Every colonel was left to act on his own.

It was three miles from Centreville to Blackburn's Ford. Near the Ford the country became wooded on the north side of Bull Run, while on the south side a rim of trees screened the open country behind. When Richardson's brigade reached the Ford, it went into battle formation in the woods. At first, the pickets could see no enemy. Then a picket saw the reflection of the sun on a rifle barrel. Another saw the gleam of a brass howitzer. A few exploratory rounds were fired with no response. Then suddenly there crashed through the leaves a volley from General James Longstreet's entire brigade. Some men of the First Massachusetts fell, and the whole Union line recoiled.

Reforming, the Federals poured a volley into the well-concealed Rebel line which broke immediately. General Longstreet said of this, "Part of my line broke and started to run. To stop the alarm, I rode with saber in hand for the leading files, determined to give them all that was in that sword and my horse's heels to stop the break." The Confederate lines were restored just in time to repulse a Union charge across the Run. Now both armies had "seen the elephant" for the first time.

Now the howitzers of the Washington Artillery of New Orleans opened on Richardson's men, driving them farther back into the woods from which it was difficult to return the fire. General Tyler appeared on the field, angry that what he had ordered as a "testing" should have turned into a minor battle. He sent back to Centreville for reserves and Ayer's battery, one of the crack artillery units of the U.S. Army.

Then there occurred one of those near-tragic errors of the kind that had happened at Big Bethel and would happen with tragic results three days hence. The First Massachusetts Infantry wore gray uniforms. A Michigan regiment, which Tyler had sent for, came up and spotting the gray uniforms, prepared to fire a volley. Fortunately the colonel of the Michigan regiment had the presence of mind to halt for a moment and yell, "Who are you?" "Massachusetts" was the answer. Later in the afternoon, a colonel in Richardson's brigade saw gray uniforms across Bull Run and thought the First Massachusetts might have succeeded in crossing. He yelled over the Run, "Who are you?" "This is who we are," came the answer, and with it a volley of Rebel rifle fire.

With the support of another brigade, Tyler tried two more assaults on Blackburn's Ford, but both times was driven back by Longstreet's rifles and the barrages of the Washington Artillery. As the afternoon wore on, the fire on both sides diminished, and finally Tyler withdrew his men. Beauregard telegraphed Jefferson Davis that a victory had been won, and Brigadier General Longstreet, who previously would have been satisfied with a paymaster's job, was a very happy man.

On July 19 and 20, Richardson's brigade returned to Blackburn's Ford, but with orders not to fire unless Longstreet attempted to cross Bull Run. The rest of McDowell's army remained in camp, receiving reinforcements from Alexandria and Arlington Heights. It was evident too that Beauregard was being reinforced, as the Federals, lying in their tents, could hear periodic train whistles on the Orange & Alexandria Railroad.

The show of force by Beauregard at Blackburn's Ford convinced McDowell that Beauregard intended to apply his strength at that point and that to attack

here might prove disastrous. Throughout July 19, McDowell sent out his engineers to see if there were any other fords across Bull Run above Stone Bridge. They found a place called Poplar Ford a mile above and west of the bridge. But a black field hand told them that a much better ford was up the Run at Mr. Sudley's mill. It was called Sudley Springs Ford. The engineers found it excellent and unguarded.

The engineers' report caused McDowell to change his entire battle plan. He would attack Beauregard's left. First he would send the rest of Tyler's division to make a feint at Blackburn's Ford. Another would make a demonstration at Stone Bridge but not attempt a crossing. The rest of his army would march to Sudley Springs Ford, swing down and cross the Warrenton Turnpike, hitting Beauregard's weak left.

On July 18, while the skirmish was going on at Blackburn's Ford, unknown to McDowell, General Johnston was unloading his first trainload of troops at the point where the Manassas Gap Railroad crossed the Warrenton Turnpike. In minutes they were on the field. Johnston went directly to Beauregard's headquarters. Now Beauregard faced the problem which had been worrying him for a month. He had planned a battle and deployed his troops. It should be "his battle." But the facts remained that Johnston outranked Beauregard and the Confederacy recognized this seniority. By the book, Beauregard should turn over the command to Johnston.

Beauregard welcomed his superior warmly, and gave him a resume of the events at Blackburn's Ford. He showed Johnston a map of the area, explaining that it did not show elevations. He added that the area was too vast for Johnston to reconnoiter in a day. When he gave Johnston his plan for the defense of Manassas Junction, Johnston admitted that he was unfamiliar with this part of Virginia, and he could not possibly suggest a battle plan without thorough reconnaissance. He ordered Beauregard to put his plan into operation. Johnston further stated that he would stand by to advise and help in any way he could.

Johnston insisted on only one point. They must go into battle on July 21. He was still convinced that Patterson's army in the Shenandoah Valley was following him, and that it could join McDowell by July 22. Therefore, if McDowell were to be defeated, it would have to be on Sunday, July 21. Throughout July 18, 19 and 20, trainloads of Johnston's troops kept arriving.

In McDowell's camp on Saturday night, July 20, the First Massachusetts had Boston baked beans as usual.

CHAPTER FIFTEEN

SUNDAY, JULY 21

ON Saturday, July 20, William Howard Russell, foreign correspondent of the London *Times,* was in the press gallery of the U.S. Senate around noon. He reported: "They drank their iced water, ate cakes or lozenges, chewed tobacco and chatted . . . as though nothing more important than a railroad bill or postal concession was being debated." He said most congressmen agreed that it would be exciting to drive out to Centreville tomorrow and see the inevitable drive for Richmond get off to a glorious start.

During the afternoon, Senator Charles Sumner of Massachusetts reported that McDowell had taken Bull Run without firing a shot and would be in Manassas Junction tomorrow. Soon afterward, John Hay, President Lincoln's secretary, appeared before the Senate and reported: "All I can tell you is that the President has heard nothing about it, and that General Scott is equally ignorant of the reported success." The senators were disappointed, but even so, they would be on hand for the glorious victory tomorrow.

SUNDAY IN CENTREVILLE

Sunday morning, July 21. Washington society and the politicians were up long before daybreak—and so were the armies of Beauregard and McDowell. Soon the caravan of coaches, landaus, cabs and buggies was on its way down the Warrenton Turnpike. The carriages were stocked for the great picnic ahead. There were demijohns of choice wine and whole country-cured Virginia hams. The hampers were packed with Chesapeake Bay oysters on ice, softshell crabs, Maryland rye whiskey, cold turkey, deviled eggs, fried chicken and cold pheasant. The atmosphere was charged with gaiety and the caravan was moving much faster than McDowell's column had done.

Arriving at Centreville, the parties got down from their carriages and spread the linen tablecloths on the grass, after having maneuvered for the best view of Bull Run. They nibbled on snacks, although they had already breakfasted, since by noon they would be too excited over McDowell's victory to eat.

The politicians were making bets on how many hours it would take for Mc-Dowell to take Manassas Junction. Senator John A. Logan had brought along a hunting rifle, hoping to get a pot shot at a Rebel at some point in the brief battle.

A man in a long grayish-white linen duster was setting up a strange-looking black box on a tripod, over which he placed a black cloth. The soldiers were later to call this apparatus the "What-is-it." The black box was a camera and the man behind it was Matthew Brady, the great portrait photographer, attempting to make his first photographic record of a battle.

It was still early morning, but in every regimental camp the bands were giving concerts. They were playing not only for the distinguished guests from Washington, but rehearsing the programs they would present in Richmond the following Sunday. The tiny hamlet of Centreville was teeming with people, but with the exception of reserve troops and regimental kitchens, all were civilians. McDowell's army had left long ago to take up its positions along Bull Run.

Arising before daybreak in the opposing camps that Sunday morning were

two officers whose names would make headlines for the next four years.

In McDowell's camp was Colonel William Tecumseh Sherman who was born in Lancaster, Ohio, in 1820. His father, a judge, died when he was nine, and he was taken into the home of an uncle, Thomas Ewing, who was an Ohio politician, soon to become a U.S. Senator. Senator Ewing obtained a West Point appointment for Sherman in 1836, and the youth graduated sixth in the class of 1840. After spending a few months on the Florida coast where he painted in watercolors while keeping one eye on the Seminoles, he was transferred to California as a lieutenant in the tiny army of occupation. Leaving the Army after the Gold Rush, he ran a bank in California for a St. Louis firm. When hard times closed the bank, Sherman became president of the Louisiana Seminary of Learning and Military Academy, which within a few years was to become Louisiana State University.

In 1861, with the secession of Louisiana approaching, Sherman resigned his presidency. With Lincoln's call for volunteers, Sherman planned to return to Ohio to accept a commission in the state militia. However, on his way he stopped at Washington to visit his brother John who was in Congress (later a candidate for the Republican Presidential nomination). John Sherman took his brother to the White House where "Cump" told President Lincoln that he would be willing to accept any command for which he was qualified. Soon the War Department commissioned him a colonel of the Thirteenth Regular Infantry. And on this Sunday morning at Centreville, William Tecumseh Sherman, who was to become a lieutenant general in four years, was commanding a brigade under McDowell.

Across Bull Run, Colonel Thomas Jonathan Jackson emerged from his tent. Jackson was born in Clarksburg, Virginia (now West Virginia) in 1824, when that section of the state was backwoods. After an extremely austere childhood, young Jackson learned from a friendly blacksmith, in 1842, that there was a West Point vacancy for his congressional district. Obtaining the appointment, because no one else in the district seemed to have wanted it, Jackson entered West Point in July of that year. Three of his classmates became Confederate generals. Like McClellan, Jackson graduated just in time to receive his commission and leave for the Mexican War as a second lieutenant. In Mexico, Jackson served with an artillery battery commanded by First Lieutenant Magruder, the "Prince John" who won the skirmish with Ben Butler at Big Bethel. Jackson came out of the war a captain. In 1851, after serving at several army posts, he was appointed Professor of Artillery Tactics and Natural Philosophy at Virginia Military Institute. Humorless, Jackson was a stern taskmaster. He was know as excessively dry and pious. Later it was said that he lived by the New Testament and fought by the Old. In January 1859 Jackson marched a battalion of his cadets to Harper's Ferry to assist Colonel Robert E. Lee in capturing John Brown. With the secession of Virginia, he received a commission as major in the Virginia State Militia. This morning at Bull Run, Jackson was a colonel in Joe Johnston's army. By nightfall, he would be "Stonewall" Jackson and, like Sherman, would later become a lieutenant general.

At 2:00 A.M., McDowell ordered Tyler's division to march to Stone Bridge. This was the first mistake of the day on the Union side. Heintzelman and Hunter were to cross Bull Run at Sudley Springs Ford and should have started first for the simple reason that they had the farthest to travel. The night was dark and Tyler's division could only feel its way along the Turnpike. To have used lanterns would have drawn the attention of the Confederate sentries. But this was also holding up Hunter and Heintzelman who were to make the major attack. Now Richardson's brigade was leaving for Blackburn's Ford unimpeded.

Finally Tyler's division, supported by Ayer's battery, went into position at Stone Bridge. But Hunter and Heintzelman, who were to have crossed Sudley Springs Ford at daybreak, 5:00 A.M., did not reach the Ford until 9:00 A.M., and then the two divisions stopped to fill their canteens and to munch on army hardtack.

Arising in Beauregard's camp at this time was E. Porter Alexander, a young Confederate officer. He was Beauregard's signal officer and with good reason. In the Old Army, Alexander had been stationed at a cavalry post in New Mexico. There he struck up a friendship with the regimental surgeon, Dr. Albert J. Myer. Myer, with a healthy regiment and time on his hands, enjoyed observing a signalling system used by the Pueblo Indians in which they transmitted messages by tipping their lances at different angles. Myer and Alexander worked out a similar system using signal flags. The army adopted the system and Dr. Myer became the first Chief of the U.S. Signal Corps. Alexander, who had been working under Myer, resigned, in order to leave the Union with his state. He was later to become Chief of the Confederate Signal Corps.

Just as Alexander was strapping his revolver to his waist, he heard the blast of a cannon. It was the first shot of the battle from Ayer's battery at Stone Bridge. There was a second shot, the scream of a cannon ball, and a hole in Captain Alexander's tent.

Down at Blackburn's Ford, Richardson's artillery had opened fire, and Beauregard believed that his prediction was right, that the attack would come there. Back at Stone Bridge, there was only the scattered firing of Tyler's pickets. Ayer's battery was silent. Hunter and Heintzelman had crossed Sudley Springs Ford, four hours late by McDowell's timetable. All was going well, but near Sudley's mill the two divisions passed the farm house of a Mr. Cunningham. As soon as the farmer identified the flag, he ran to his barn, mounted his horse and took off in the direction of Manassas Junction. At the Warrenton Turnpike, he turned left toward Stone Bridge where Evans's brigade was stationed.

Reaching Evans, Cunningham told him what he had seen and that momentarily two Federal divisions would be in his rear. Most seasoned commanders are skeptical when they get reports of troop strength from a civilian. Too often he reports a brigade to be a division and a company a regiment.

But the fact that Cunningham had seen Federal troops on the road from Sudley Springs to the Turnpike meant that, regardless of their strength, they would be at Evans's rear and could outflank the entire Confederate position.

Now Evans was in a dilemma. If he changed his position to the intersection of the Sudley Springs road and the Turnpike, he would leave Stone Bridge unprotected. Since there had been only light fire from across the Run, Evans could not judge the opposing strength. If he could place his troops at the Turnpike intersection he might be able to hold off an attack from both the Sudley Springs road and Stone Bridge *if* St. George Cocke's brigade, just below at Lewis Ford, would form a line with him. But this would require an order from Beauregard, and Beauregard was still concentrating on Blackburn's Ford. Evans made a snap decision and, without orders, pulled his brigade back to meet the assault from Sudley Springs. However, in his haste, he failed to send a courier to Beauregard with a description of the situation.

Evans's decision would have proved fatal had Tyler acted as recklessly as he had on the July 18 at Blackburn's Ford. The combined forces of Evans's brigade and Cocke's could not have stood against three divisions, 6,000 against 18,000. But Tyler did not move, and Ayer's battery fired round after round at a brigade which was no longer there.

Now the two divisions from Sudley Springs were approaching the Turnpike. Former Colonel Burnside, now a brigadier general, took the lead with an oversize brigade of 4,000 men from Hunter's division. They left the Sudley Springs road, fanning out into the woods and underbrush with the Second Rhode Island as skirmishers. The men were jittery; they had not seen the elephant. Prudently seeking shelter, they slowed the advance. This was not what they had expected of war. This was like hunting a rabbit who had a gun. The flag was not leading a wild charge; its folds were caught in a briar bush. There was no martial music to stir the blood.

Finally the skirmishers of the Second Rhode Island emerged into waist-high grass just to the west of the stone house and the turnpike. Evans's brigade opened a scattering fire—no volleys because the Rhode Islanders were spread out. Each Johnny Reb picked his Yank. But the ancient smoothbore muskets were inaccurate at this range and did little damage except to give the skirmishers the experience of hearing the whines of very close bullets.

Hunter's division emerged from the woods into an open field, an ideal location for a charge. Had Hunter swept down on Evans's brigade, that part of the battle would have been over very quickly. In the close-formation charges of those days, momentum was very important. Unless faced with overwhelming odds, the well-executed charge just kept going. Also it kept up morale, since the soldier running forward had no time to see how many of his comrades were dropping. But Hunter stopped his division just to the rear of the Second Rhode Island. This delay permitted the brigades of Bee and Bartow, plus six regiments of Johnston's men, to come to the support of Evans. They were followed by Imboden's battery with four guns.

During this action, all was confusion along the rest of the Confederate lines, caused by a long series of vague, contradictory orders issued by Beauregard. Despite a signal tower set up by Alexander, communications with Beauregard's headquarters had all but broken down. Orders were written which never reached the field officers. Beauregard thought that General Richard Stoddert Ewell was across Bull Run at Union Mills Ford. Ewell was standing still. General D.R. Jones was believed to be across Bull Run supporting Ewell. Instead, Jones was waiting to hear that Ewell had crossed. It was assumed that Longstreet had crossed the Run and was supporting Ewell and Jones. Longstreet had crossed but, without further orders, was only skirmishing with the enemy.

At this point, Beauregard received a message from Captain Alexander's signal tower that there was a large cloud of dust over the Warrenton Turnpike and heavy firing. Johnston was afraid that the attacking force was Patterson's army from the Shenandoah which would add 22,000 men to McDowell's army. Strangely, this unexpected attack on the left failed to perturb Beauregard, who did not even ride out to see what was happening. Then a messenger from Union Mills Ford brought the news that Beauregard's orders had not been delivered and Ewell wanted to know what to do. Now Beauregard realized that the offensive he had so carefully planned on his right was a thing of the past.

Back at the Turnpike, Confederate arms were taking a severe toll of Union officers. The militia officers, under fire for the first time, seem to have been acting out the fanciful picture of pre-Napoleonic battles when an officer seized the flag in one hand, waved his sword in the direction of the enemy and led the charge in front of his regiment. General Hunter was severely wounded by a piece of shrapnel and two colonels in Burnside's brigade were killed. Now two Union batteries of six guns each galloped up, unlimbered and went into action. The Rebels fell back.

At Beauregard's headquarters, Johnston was pacing the floor and biting his tongue. The roar of battle on the Confederate left was heightening. But Johnston had promised to let Beauregard run the show. Beauregard, noticing Johnston's nervous tension, sent six couriers with a staff officer to the left with orders to report every ten minutes. The first courier reported that the Federals were felling trees for fortifications along the Turnpike. Johnston could stand it no longer. He waved his hat in the direction of the dust and smoke and snapped, "The battle is there. I'm going!"

Now Hunter's division was joined by Heintzelman's. Sherman's brigade followed, with more artillery. They had been delayed as a result of the bottleneck created by Tyler's division at Stone Bridge.

The Federal fire power was now so strong that the Rebel line could not withstand it, and the brigades were drawn back from the Turnpike up a gentle slope to the Henry house, which still stands. This was the scene that greeted

Johnston as he rode up. All along the way he had come upon detachments and batteries, unengaged and without orders. These he hurried into action. At the battle line, he found utter confusion. Units were broken and so mingled that few privates knew the commanders they were fighting under. This was a common condition in the early battles of the war. Demoralized men straggled to the rear, regained confidence and joined new units coming up. After a battle it took days to get the men back into the companies in which they had enlisted.

Beauregard joined Johnston after renewing his orders to Longstreet, Ewell and Jones to cross Bull Run at Mitchell's and Blackburn's fords, to try to press a counterattack against Centreville, but at least to silence the Union batteries. It was now 12:30 P.M. and the fighting had been going on for approximately three hours. Beauregard placed himself in command of the right of the line toward the Run and asked Johnston to take the left. The immediate danger was that the Yanks would sweep around the left and cut off the road to Manassas Junction.

Desperately Beauregard and Johnston tried to restore the shattered lines, but it appeared that all was lost. Every Union charge up the slope toward the Henry house further demoralized the Rebs. The remnants of companies decimated by artillery fire were wandering back to shelter. Suddenly there was a glimmer of encouragement. The Hampton Legion of South Carolina, under the command of Wade Hampton, the richest and most cultured man in the state, came on the field fresh and finely equipped.

Beauregard began calling in troops from the center of his line to reinforce his left above the Turnpike. These troops had been engaged only lightly and were relatively fresh. St. George Cocke came from Lewis Ford, Bonham from Mitchell's Ford and from McLean's Ford came Thomas Jonathan Jackson.

Both Beauregard and Johnston, and their staffs, frantically rode up and down the lines, pulling commands together, rounding up stragglers and pressing into action commands which had not been engaged. Over the crest of the hill they found the fourth Alabama. At the moment it was unofficered and had not fired a shot all day. Johnston scooped up a young boy who was the flag bearer, placed the boy behind him on his horse, and led the regiment to the battle line. There he placed it under Jackson's command. After an hour of continuous effort, Beauregard and Johnston had the Confederate line strengthened to a point where it was able to repulse the next union charge up the slope.

It was during this assault that the "Stonewall" Jackson legend originated. Jackson's Virginia Brigade bore the brunt of the attack, while others were falling back, including General Bee's troops. To rally his men, Bee is said to have called out, "See Jackson standing like a stone wall." Another legend, less well known, involved Jackson's forefinger being nicked by a bullet at this crucial time. To slow the bleeding, he is supposed to have raised his arm with his finger pointing upward. It was said by those who saw him that he had pronounced a blessing on his troops which made them more steadfast than ever.

Now Beauregard displayed a curious twist of his Creole mind. Just at the moment when Johnston had stepped in and temporarily saved the day, Beauregard asked him to retire. Johnston was affronted and, for the first time, reminded Beauregard that he was his senior in command. Beauregard insisted that since he had drafted the orders for the battle, and they had been approved by Johnston, it was his responsibility to carry them out and accept the resulting blame or credit. Further, Beauregard said there was a need for a supreme commander on the battle line, and another at the rear to rush reinforcements to their proper assignments. The reinforcements to which Beauregard referred were the regiments of Johnston's rear guard in the Shenandoah Valley. They had been scheduled to arrive on Saturday but on Sunday they were missing and had not been heard from. Sullenly Johnston accepted Beauregard's "logic" and withdrew to the Lewis farm, somewhat to the east of the Henry house.

Actually, this was a wise move by Beauregard. The Lewis house was on the road to Manassas Junction, and all troops coming from that direction would pass by. Also, since it was on high ground, Johnston could watch the progress at Mitchell's and Blackburn's fords and still keep one eye on the Warrenton Turnpike north of Stone Bridge.

Now there was a brief change in Beauregard's luck. The fighting had lulled momentarily, giving Beauregard a chance to ride up and down the line, encouraging the men and promising them that help was on the way. Suddenly, without orders, Colonel A.C. Cummings of the thirty-third Virginia sent his men into a wild charge. The Virginia men tore into the Union line, catching it completely off guard. This was the first time that day that any Confederate unit had taken the offensive. The Virginians all but pushed the Federals off the plateau. Aided by a cross fire from Jackson's brigade, they captured two fine artillery batteries and turned the guns on the Federals. Cheers went up along the Rebel line, but they were premature. The Union line reformed, pushed up the slope and recovered its artillery.

Now came one of those unforseeable events that can completely reverse the fortunes of war.

McDowell, in violation of acceptable military tactics of the time, ordered Griffin's and Ricketts' batteries placed in advance of the infantry line for more effective shelling of the area around the Henry house. Ricketts objected strenuously and demanded infantry support. But he was a Regular Army man, long accustomed to obeying unpleasant orders, and he advanced his guns.

Then, just south of the artillery position, a regiment appeared in gray uniforms. Major Barry, McDowell's chief of artillery, who was with Griffin's and Ricketts' batteries, insisted that they were Union troops coming to support the batteries. Ricketts contended that they were Rebels, ordered his guns swung around and loaded with double cannister. Barry was angry and called Ricketts' attention to the flag. It was a stifling day and there was no breeze. The flag hung limp but at a distance there appeared to be red and white stripes and a blue field. Ricketts swung his guns back to play on the Henry house.

At this point in the war, the Confederacy had not yet adopted what became its familiar battle flag. The Confederate flag at Bull Run had three broad stripes, red, white and red and a blue field with the stars of the eleven Confederate states. Hanging limp, it was almost impossible to distinguish from the United States flag.

Now the troops in gray entered the woods on the east side of the Turnpike as if they were going to skirmish with Beauregard's left. The two batteries kept up their incessant shelling of the Confederate line. Then a regiment in gray emerged from the woods at the same point where one in gray had entered. The flag still hung limp. Major Barry naturally took it for granted that this was the same regiment he had seen enter the woods. It looked the same in every detail. The regiment marched down the Turnpike toward the two batteries as though it were in a Fourth of July parade. Then it wheeled and halted. The colonel walked up and down the ranks talking to the men. He stepped aside and raised his sword. The rifles came up and the colonel's sword came down. There was a blinding volley and nearly every man in the two batteries was dead. The regiment was the advance guard of Johnston's last brigade out of the Valley. The brigade had detrained where the Manassas Gap Railroad crossed the Turnpike and run all the way.

The New York Fire Zouaves charged in to rescue the guns of the two batteries. But there was another volley from the new regiment and another from up on the slope. The Zouaves were thus caught in a cross fire and were decimated. Those who had not fallen broke and ran. Now the rest of the brigade from the Shenandoah came on the field. Up at the Henry house, men who had felt their cause was hopeless and who were ready to throw down their guns and go home now were tigers. The blood-curdling "Rebel yell" went up and down the line. Then came the last straw for the Federals. Roaring down the pike came Jeb Stuart's cavalry, waving their sabers and shooting their revolvers in the air. Men who had fought bravely all day, who had stood and taken volley after volley of rifle fire, who had withstood barrages of cannister and grape shot, were now terrified by this legendary Black Horse Cavalry.

Everything went to pieces at once. Discipline vanished, and officers' commands were empty words. There was no such thing as authority. Some regiments remained intact and retreated by the route they had come, Sudley Springs Ford, but most were no longer units. It was every man for himself, and the shortest way to Washington was over Stone Bridge, which immediately was completely clogged. Then Jeb Stuart's cavalry and the Nineteenth Virginia sealed off Sudley Springs.

Beauregard, who had been on the defensive all day, and who had long since thrown away his plan of battle, was unprepared for this sudden collapse of McDowell's army. He could have ordered Longstreet's and Bonham's brigades to advance from Mitchell's and Blackburn's fords to advance on Centreville to cut off the Union retreat, but he had his hands full at the Henry house and communications were not sufficient to change anything now. Then, to crown the victory, President Jefferson Davis appeared on the field, having come from Richmond by special train.

To the north of Bull Run, everything was chaos and panic. The Turnpike was hopelessly clogged. In the mad gallop for Washington, the carriages of the "visitors' gallery" were overturned and one congressman was taken prisoner by a Rebel company. Teamsters in the wagon trains cut their horses' harnesses, left the wagons in the road and rode their nags toward Arlington. With the Turnpike thus blocked, artillery had to be abandoned to the Confederates. Musicians of the regimental bands, who had been left at Centreville during the battle, mounted the artillery horses and clung on.

McDowell's first thought was to make a stand at Centreville. It provided a good defensive position, and he had converted the Confederate barricades into a strong bastion. But although he had more than enough men, he did not have an army or even a brigade. What remained were some 27,000 panicked individuals who could not have found their companies if they had wanted to. Furthermore, all his troops had been engaged in a constant offensive since 9:30 that Sunday morning. They had eaten only a bite of tough, tasteless army hardtack, and their canteens were empty. They were in no condition to continue fighting, and it was now 5:00 P.M.

The Rebels were in like condition, except in organization. Their army was still intact. They followed the Union retreat as far as Centreville and found the village empty. There they followed the good old New England custom of eating warmed-over baked beans on Sunday, thanks to the First Massachusetts. Here and there was a half of a choice Virginia ham, left by an Illinois senator's wife, part of a demijohn of wine, and a pheasant breast. Then it began to rain.

Few of the Confederate troops had witnessed the arrival of President Davis at Bull Run. Although a former army officer and Secretary of War, he refrained from telling Johnston or Beauregard what he would do if he were in their position. Toward sundown, Davis finally called a council of war to decide on an immediate march on Washington. The consensus, which included Davis, was that the army was exhausted and had insufficient materials. Also, it was necessary to collect and dispose of the Confederate dead, to make provision for the wounded, and to gather together the wealth of equipment and supplies left by the retreating Federals. In any event, with a drizzling rain, the Warrenton Turnpike would be a quagmire as soon as an army started to move over it. It was decided that to occupy Centreville was enough.

The Confederate generals returned to their brigades, and Jefferson Davis rode to the Orange & Alexandria railroad station. There he penned a telegram to the people of the Confederacy through the Confederate Congress at Richmond: "Night has closed on a hard fought field. Our forces were victorious. The enemy was routed and fled precipitately, abandoning a large amount of arms, ammunition, knapsacks and baggage. The ground was strewn for miles with those killed, and the farmhouses and the ground around were filled with wounded.

"Pursuit was continued along several routes toward Leesburg and Centreville until darkness covered the fugitives. We have captured several field batteries, stands of arms, and Union and state flags. Many prisoners have been taken. Too high praise cannot be bestowed, whether for the skill of the principal officers or for the gallantry of all our troops. The battle was fought mainly on our left."

Casualty figures for Bull Run vary according to historians and where they lived, but an average indicates that between 1,800 and 2,000 were killed or wounded on both sides that bloody Sunday.

CHAPTER SIXTEEN

AT THE SPOTSWOOD AND WILLARD'S

IT rained in both Washington and Richmond on Monday, July 22. At the Spotswood Hotel in Richmond, the bar was filled with a crowd of men, most of whom had been there all night. They were hoarse from cheering the news from Manassas Junction, and they were grabbing up every new newspaper edition to learn if Beauregard had taken Washington yet. Some were of the opinion that after Beauregard had chased the Yankees out of Maryland, a peace treaty would be signed on the banks of the Schuylkill River just outside Philadelphia, and everything below that point would belong to the confederacy.

There were new heroes, virtually unknown before the battle: Stonewall Jackson, Wade Hampton, Longstreet, Bonham, St. George Cocke, Wheat of the Louisiana Tigers, Evans, and Bee (who had been killed). And now the crowd thought that Beauregard *must* be the reincarnation of Napoleon. The front page of the Richmond *Examiner* carried a letter from Jefferson Davis to Beauregard:

> Sir,—Appreciating your services in the battle of Manassas and on several other occasions during the existing war, as affording the highest evidence of your skill as a commander, your gallantry as a soldier and your zeal as a patriot, you are appointed to be "General" in the Army of the Confederate States of America, and, with the consent of Congress, will be duly commissioned accordingly.
>
> Yours, etc.
>
> Jefferson Davis

Now the crowd braved the rain and poured out on the sidewalk to jeer a company of Yankee prisoners who were marching under guard. But their jeers were soon stilled when the prisoners were followed by a hearse bearing the body of General Bee, the first high-ranking officer of the Confederacy to be killed in battle.

Then came the crushing news that Beauregard was still at Centreville and had made no attempt to pursue McDowell into Washington. The Great Creole was no longer the reincarnation of Napoleon. What was the matter with Jeff Davis—he could have made Bory press on. Why let the army lie down when it was winning? A carload of Confederate caskets was unloaded at the railroad station. The Monday morning generals were hushed again. At noon, President Davis came down to the Spotswood for dinner with Secretary of War Benjamin. He looked confident but not elated. Only the privileged few spoke with him, and history has not recorded what was said.

At the bar of Willard's Hotel in Washington there was also a crowd which had been there all night receiving the conflicting reports from Centreville. Those picnickers who had left the battlefield early in the afternoon reported a crushing defeat of the Confederacy. Then came a message from McDowell that he had met with reverses and was falling back on Centreville. The next message put the withdrawal at Fairfax Court House. And finally came a telegram that McDowell was marching to Washington.

Now added to the crowd which had kept the vigil during the night were dozens of bedraggled army officers, drenched to the skin from the "march" back from Centreville. Mingled with them were a number of grim congressmen who had yelled, "On to Richmond," on Saturday and who had whipped their horses all the way back from Bull Run. They told of Congressman Nye who had lingered over his cold pheasant too long and was now a prisoner in Richmond. The officers, mostly of the volunteer militia, were a confused lot. They should have been with their commands, but where were the commands? Units had become so hopelessly intermingled that it would take days to reassemble them.

London *Times* correspondent William Howard Russell described the morning scene outside on Pennsylvania Avenue: "I saw a steady stream of men covered with mud, soaked through with rain, who were pouring irregularly, without any sense of order, up Pennsylvania Avenue toward the Capitol. A dense stream of vapor rose from the multitude, but looking closely at the men, I perceived they belonged to different regiments mingled pell-mell together."

Now into the barroom came Matthew Brady in his sopping-wet linen duster. He had lost everything—his horse, his wagon and his camera. Under his duster he wore a sword which an officer of the New York Fire Zouaves had thrown away in flight.

From across the Potomac came the news that every church in Alexandria had been taken over as a hospital. The one exception was Christ Church (Episcopalian), because George Washington's pew was still there. Word also came that John Cameron, brother of the Secretary of War, had been killed. A crowd outside Willard's tried to organize a lynching party to hang a troop of Confederate prisoners.

The city expected to be invaded at any moment. Free blacks were leaving, because they feared capture as runaway slaves, which they were not. President Lincoln called upon General Scott to organize a defense, but the old man was too feeble to do anything about it. Then came word from McDowell that he was in Arlington with enough regiments intact to hold out in the fortification. But confidence in McDowell was rapidly fading, and few were cheered by the news.

All day the exhausted troops straggled into Washington. They had fought hard all the day before and then had walked all night without rest or food. They flopped down on doorsteps in the rain and slept. They pulled doorbells and begged for food and they stumbled into Willard's bar for stimulants. Their Fourth of July uniforms were falling apart, and many were shoeless. But their three months were up and they were going home. Most had had enough of war and couldn't care less whether the Rebels took Washington or not. But there were others who were going home to re-enlist in the regular army for the duration. Lincoln would immediately send out a call for 300,000 volunteers.

The dejected officers in Willard's bar alibied the defeat. Rightfully, they blamed the newspapers, especially Greeley's New York *Tribune,* and the politicians, for driving Lincoln to order an advance when the army was in no way prepared except in supply. Also they rightly blamed the ill-trained militia officers who had obtained their commissions through personal popularity rather than military experience. Many were now agreed that Richmond could never be taken; that Lincoln should have a conference with Jefferson Davis and call the whole thing off.

But one man, who was in Washington as part-time male army nurse, part-

Walt Whitman

time war correspondent, but mostly poet, took a dim view of all army brass at the moment. Walt Whitman was in Willard's bar on the night of July 22. He had little to add to what had already been said about the defeat, but in his journal for that date he made this entry:

"I see them and must have a word with them. There you are, shoulder straps!—But where are your companies? Where are your men? Incompetents! Never tell me of the chance of battle, of getting strayed, and the like. I think this is your work, this retreat, after all. Sneak, blow, put on airs here in Willard's sumptous parlors and barrooms or anywhere—no explanation shall save you. Bull Run is your work; had you been half or one-tenth worthy as your men, this never would have happened."

BIBLIOGRAPHY

BIBLIOGRAPHY

Abbott, John S.C. *The History of the Civil War in America.* 2 vols. Springfield, Mass.: Gurdon Hill, 1863.

Armstrong, James Borden. *General Simon Goodell Griffin's Account of Nelson and the New Hampshire Militia.* New Hampshire Historical Society, vol. XXI, No. 2, Concord, N.H.: 1966.

Bettersworth, John K. *Confederate Mississippi.* Baton Rouge: Louisiana State University Press, 1943.

Billings, John D. *Hardtack and Coffee, The Unwritten Story of Army Life.* Boston: George M. Smith & Co., 1887.

Butler, Benjamin F. *Butler's Book.* Boston: A.M. Thayer, 1892.

Cameron, Simon, Secretary of War. *U.S. Army Regulations 1861.* Washington, D.C.: Government Printing Office, 1861.

Chapel, Charles E. *Gun Collecting.* New York: Coward McCann, 1939.

Chestnut, Mary Boykin. *My Diary from Dixie,* edited by Ben Ames Williams. Boston: Houghton Mifflin, 1949.

Coffin, Charles Carleton. *Drum-beat of the Nation.* New York: Harper & Bros., 1888.

Cudworth, Warren H. *Histroy of the First Massachusetts Infantry.* Boston: Walker, Fuller & Co., 1866.

Davis, Varina Howell. *Jefferson Davis—A Memoir By His Wife.* 2 vols. New York: Belford Publishers, 1890.

Eckenrode, H.J., and Conrad, Bryan. *James Longstreet, Lee's War Horse,* Chapel Hill: University of North Carolina Press, 1936.

Foster, G. Allen. *The Eyes and Ears of the Civil War.* New York: Criterion Books, 1963.

Freeman, Douglas Southall. *Lee's Lieutenants.* 3 vols. New York: Charles Scribner's Sons, 1942.

————. *R.E. Lee.* 4 vols. New York: Charles Scribner's Sons, 1941.

Greeley, Horace. *The American Conflict.* 2 vols. Hartford, Conn.: O.D. Case, 1864.

Helper, Hinton Rowan. *The Impending Crisis.* New York: Burdick Brothers, 1857.

Henderson, Colonel G.F.R. *Stonewall Jackson and the American Civil War.* New York: Grossett & Dunlap [date of authorized American edition not listed].

Hendrick, Burton J. *Statesmen of the Lost Cause.* Boston: Little Brown, 1939.

Karsner, David. *John Brown, Terrible Saint.* New York: Dodd, Mead, 1934.

Leech, Margaret. *Reveille in Washington.* New York: Harper & Brothers, 1941.

Logan, John A. *The Great Conspiracy.* New York: A.R. Hart, 1886.

Lowenfels, Walter. *Walt Whitman's Civil War.* New York: Alfred A. Knopf, 1960.

McClellan, George B. *McClellan's Own Story.* New York: Charles L. Webster, 1887.

Pollard, Edward A. *The Lost Cause.* New York: E.B. Treat, 1867.

Poore, Benjamin Perley. *The Life and Public Services of Ambrose E. Burnside.* Providence, R.I.: J.A. & R.A. Reid, 1882.

————. *Perley's Reminiscences.* Philadelphia: Hubbard Brothers, 1886.

Pryor, Mrs. Roger A. *Reminiscences of War and Peace.* New York: Grosset & Dunlap, 1904.

BIBLIOGRAPHY

Richardson, James D. *Messages and Papers of the Confederacy.* 2 vols. Nashville, Tenn.: United States Publishing Co., 1905.

Russell, William Howard. *British War Correspondent.* Boston: T.O.H.F. Burnham, 1863.

Schouler, William. *Massachusetts in the Civil War.* 2 vols. Published by the author, Boston, 1871.

Sherman, William Tecumseh. *Memoirs of Gen. W.T. Sherman.* New York: Charles L. Webster & Co., 1891.

Stephens, Alcxander H. *A Constitutional View of the War Between the States.* Philadelphia: National Publishing Co., 1868.

Swinton, William. *Campaigns of the Army of the Potomac.* New York: Charles D. Richardson, 1866.

Trobriand, Regis de. *Four Years with the Army of the Potomac.* Boston: Ticknor & Co., 1889.

Wiley, Bell Irvin. *The Life of Johnny Reb, The Common Soldier of the Confederacy.* New York: Bobbs-Merrill, 1943.

INDEX